Sports Starters

Tennis

TERRY MABBITT

COLLINS
Glasgow & London

First published 1979
Reprinted 1981
by William Collins Sons and Company Limited,
Glasgow and London
© 1979 William Collins Sons and Company Limited

Devised, edited and designed by Youé and Spooner Limited
Special photography by John McGovren
Illustrations by John Jamieson and Malcolm Studio
Filmset by Photocomp Limited
Colour processing by Medway Reprographic Limited

ISBN 0 00 411611 9

Printed in Great Britain

Contents

Introduction

My aim in this book is to show how all the members of the family (from about age four upwards) can learn to play and enjoy tennis – I say show because in this different type of tennis book a lot of the instruction is visual. You should be able to take the book on court with you and from its step-by-step diagrams and pictures improve your technique on the spot. (Although I suggest you consult it while practising rather than between points in a game!)

I myself started to play tennis when I was fourteen – considered fairly late, these days – and it played an important part in my leisure activities. Bedfordshire, England, was my home county; I was captain of tennis there for ten years and in eight of them, county champion. In 1979 I reached the semi-final of the National County Champions tournament. Tennis and squash often go hand in hand and I am also a qualified squash professional, county champion seven times.

In 1968 the greatest of all tennis tournaments, Wimbledon, was the first to go 'open' – to allow professionals to compete. This gave a great boost to professionals and to tennis, and the fact that coaches could now compete in local and county events was a factor in my decision to change my career from commerce to sport. On passing the Lawn Tennis Association's professional's exam in 1972, I became county coach for Bedfordshire and Northamptonshire; for two years I was a West Midlands Regional Coach before moving to Yorkshire in 1978 to become North East Regional Coach and Ilkley Club professional. The club has two fine indoor courts so that we can play even in the thickest snowstorm and many of the indoor pictures used in this book were taken there.

All this adds up to a lot of playing and coaching experience, and I hope some of it comes through in the pages that follow. I know the beginner's difficulties and the regular player's hang-ups. I receive a great deal of satisfaction both from teaching youngsters to play tennis and from helping players who have played for many years and need new ideas and some unique techniques improved.

Left: Margaret Court demonstrates the power and grace which brought her three Wimbledon singles championships. Far right: Jimmy Connors, another Wimbledon champion, playing all out. Near right: myself, helping a youngster to do it the right, and so the easiest, way

The production of this book has demanded a good deal of patience from all concerned and I would like to thank my designers, Trevor Spooner and Ian Hughes, plus my editor, Angela Wyatt, who has had the task of reducing my enthusiastic manuscript to order. I am also very grateful to the various players we used in the photographs, including my fellow professionals and many friends.

Jerry Mabbutt

Getting to know the game

All you need initially is a racket, balls and tennis shoes, plus an opponent. Before you buy a racket, I suggest you read the section on equipment on page 104. It is also a good idea to acquire a basic knowledge of the game before starting to play.

Tennis can be played by two opposing people (singles) or by opposing pairs (doubles). The aim, of course, is to hit the ball over the net and within the boundaries of the court. The ball can bounce once before it is hit, or not bounce at all.

The diagram opposite shows the lines of the court. The only difference in its use between singles and doubles is that, in singles, the court area is bounded by the singles side lines. A ball that falls outside the base or side line is out of play; one that falls actually on the line is still in play.

The game starts with one player serving the ball from behind the base line on the right-hand side of the centre mark into the service box diagonally opposite (the area bounded by centre line, service line and singles side line). If his first ball falls outside this area or does not clear the net, this is a 'fault' and he has a second try. If he fails again (a double fault), the point goes to his opponent. If the ball falls in the correct service box but hits the net first (a 'let'), it does not count (though if it touches the net at any other time, it remains in play) and the server is allowed that service again. The player receiving the service must let the ball bounce before he hits it back, and the rally continues until the point is won. For the second point, the server serves from the left of the centre mark into the other, diagonally opposite, service box; he serves into alternate boxes until the game is over, when it is his opponent's turn to serve. The players change court ends on every odd game.

Before the game, there is a toss-up for choice of service or end. If the winner chooses to serve, his opponent can choose at which end he starts to play. Instead of tossing a coin and calling heads or tails, a racket is spun and the call is 'rough' or 'smooth'. If you look at the racket strings, you will normally find at the top and bottom a thinner, extra string. Its knotted side is 'rough', the smooth side 'smooth'.

In scoring, the server's score is called first followed by his opponent's. The numbers called bear no relation to the points won! The score mounts thus: love (which is nought), fifteen, thirty, forty, game. If forty-all is reached, it is called deuce and two clear points must then be won, otherwise the score returns to deuce. Points after deuce are called advantage ('advantage server' or 'advantage receiver'). The first to score six games wins the set, unless five-all is reached when two clear games have to be won. In theory, the number of games to a set is thus infinite, so some tournaments use tie-breaks (see page 124). A match usually consists of the best of three sets, though some men's matches are the best of five.

Before going on to a court, you can get the feel of the ball by hitting it against a wall or having someone throw balls to you (see page 14), maybe in the back garden.

Turn to page 20 to find the right way to hold your racket.

▲ The Wimbledon scoreboard is explicit – games in previous sets, names, server indicated by a dash against the name, sets, games in this set and current score

◄ A famous occasion: Buster Mottram (GB) serves to John McEnroe (USA) in the 1978 Davis Cup final at Palm Springs

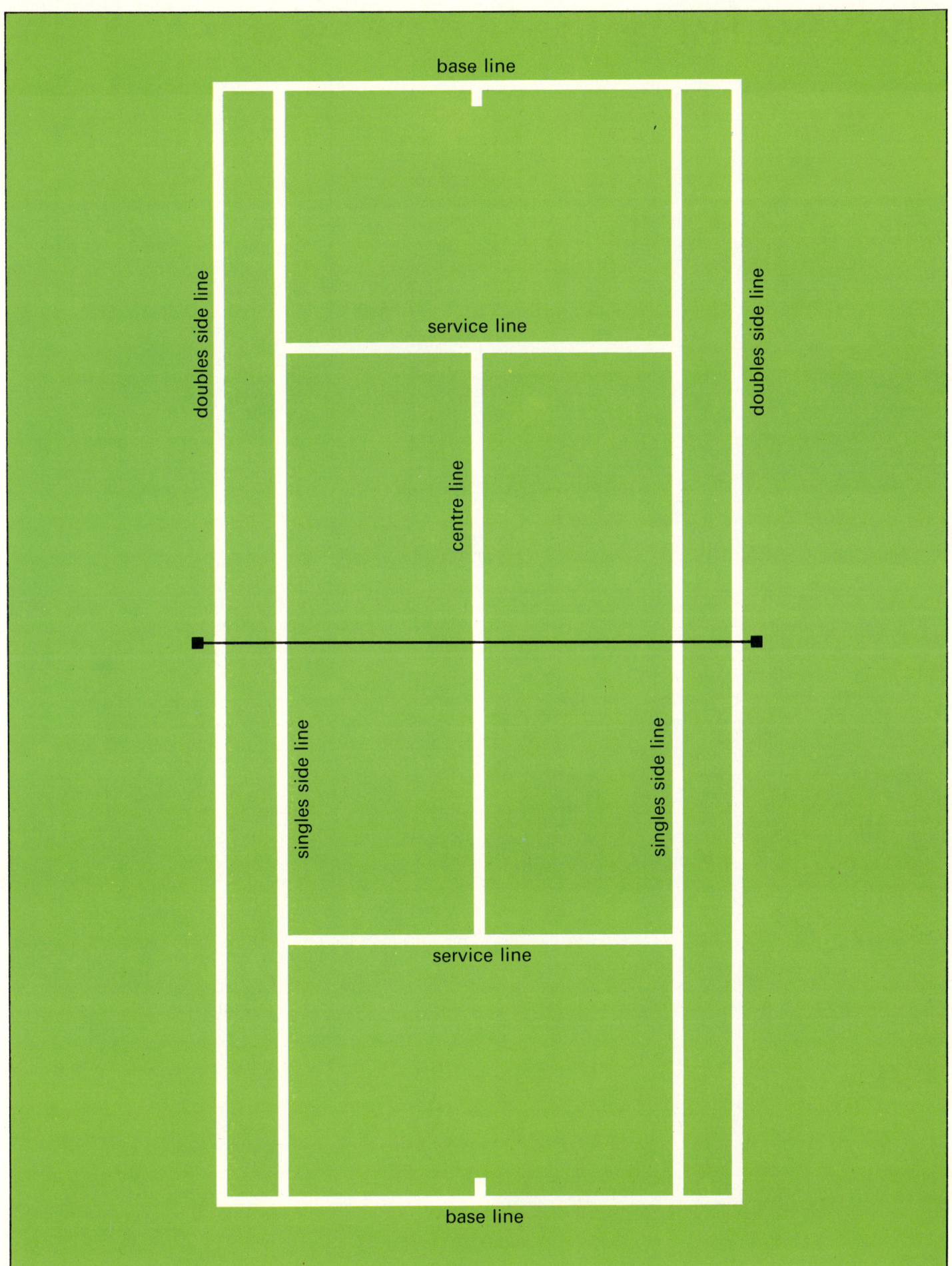

The singles game

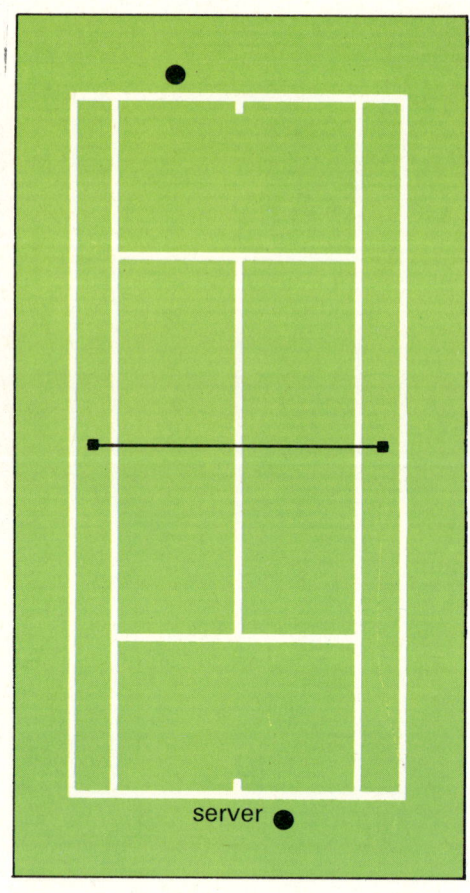

▲ As in doubles, in singles the player serving serves alternately from right and left to the diagonally opposite service box, and so in singles the receiver moves too

The black dots show the players' positions in singles when the service is to the forehand court (receiver's right hand). The singles court is bounded by the inner side lines and base lines ▶

server ●

▲ Singles is an individualistic game and is inclined to keep you warmer than a doubles game!

Singles Your first aim is to hit more balls into court than your opponent, that is, aim for consistency rather than the spectacular. The basic shot involves hitting the ball deep to the back of the court, which puts your opponent under pressure. If he is at the back of the court, you can safely give the ball some height over the net, which will also give you a better length.

You should try to vary your game with deep, short or wide balls and to vary the pace and spin given to the ball. You should learn to volley (hit the ball before it bounces), and attack as well as defend with ground strokes (balls hit after a bounce) and lobs (balls hit high in the air). These strokes need practice and your main consideration should be to play within your capabilities in matches, meanwhile increasing your repertoire of strokes in practice sessions.

Doubles There are many examples of pairs who, individually, would often lose but, because of the way they combine in doubles, can often beat their opponents. Doubles is a much more systematic game than singles, with a basic pattern of hitting the ball diagonally across court.

At the beginning of each set, each pair must decide in which order they will receive service;

The doubles game

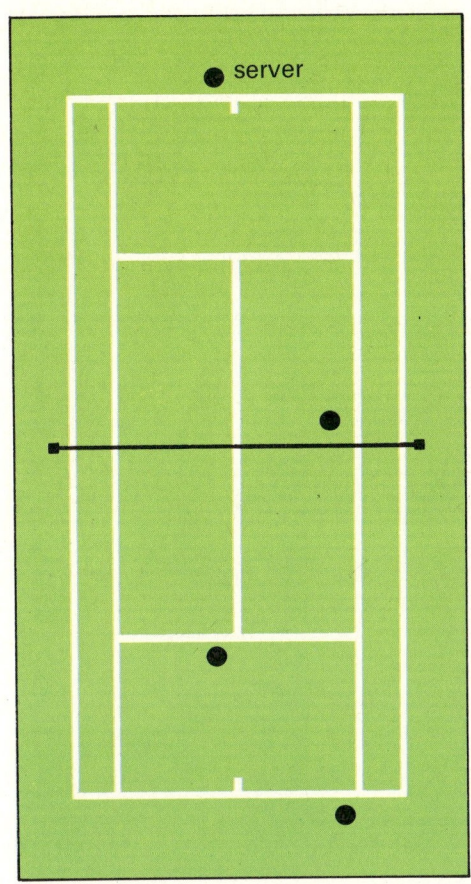

◀ The black dots show the players' positions in doubles when the service is to the forehand court. The space between the inner and outer side lines ('tramlines') is now in use

▲ A friendly game of doubles with three of the players standing back. As your standard improves, you should try to move in to the net as quickly as you are able

in effect, whether to play on the left or the right. It is important that you become capable of playing well on either side. At the beginning of each set, each pair decides who will serve first and this order is kept.

The player receiving service should stand just behind the base line in about the centre of his half of the court, and move in a couple of paces for a weaker second service. His partner should stand just behind the service line ready to move back and join his partner if he plays a poor return or to go forward to the net if he plays a good one.

The server's partner should stand a racket length and a pace back from the net in the middle of his half of the court, ready to cut off a weak return with a volley.

When the service is to the receiver's left, or backhand, court, the server should stand nearer the 'tramlines' (side lines) to get a better angle to the receiver's usually weaker backhand and to cover his own on the return.

A basic tactic for the beginner to remember is that if he is lobbed while at the net and his partner runs behind him to play the ball, he should cross over to cover the half of the court left undefended by his partner.

▲ A pair who combine better, rather than the pair who are the best players individually, will win at doubles

13

Ball sense

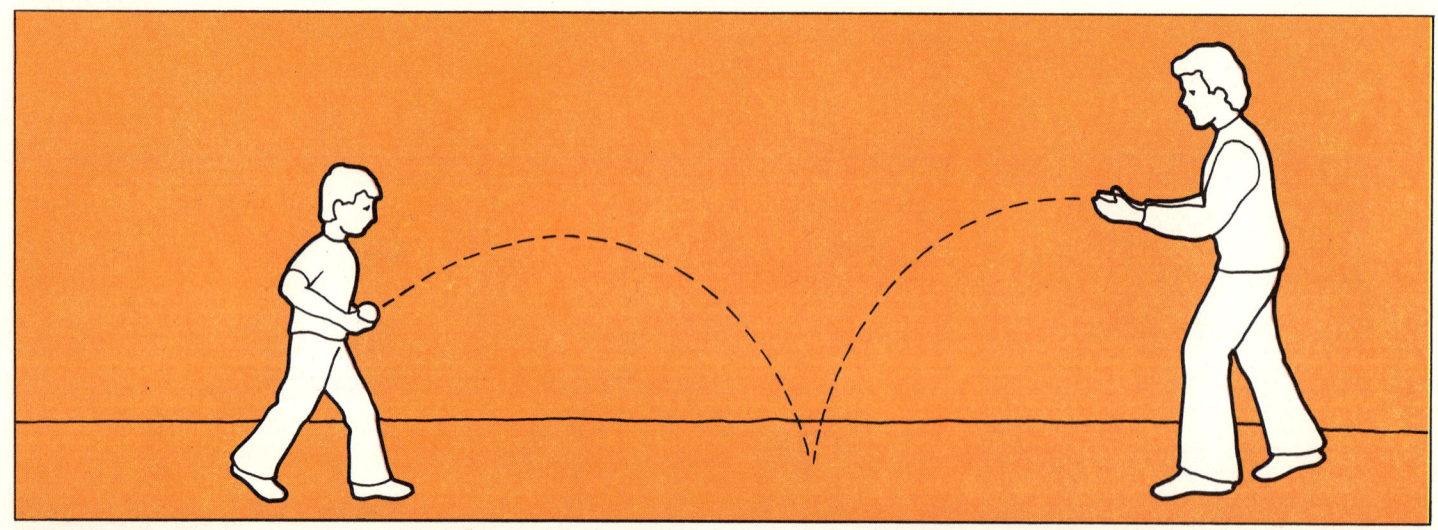

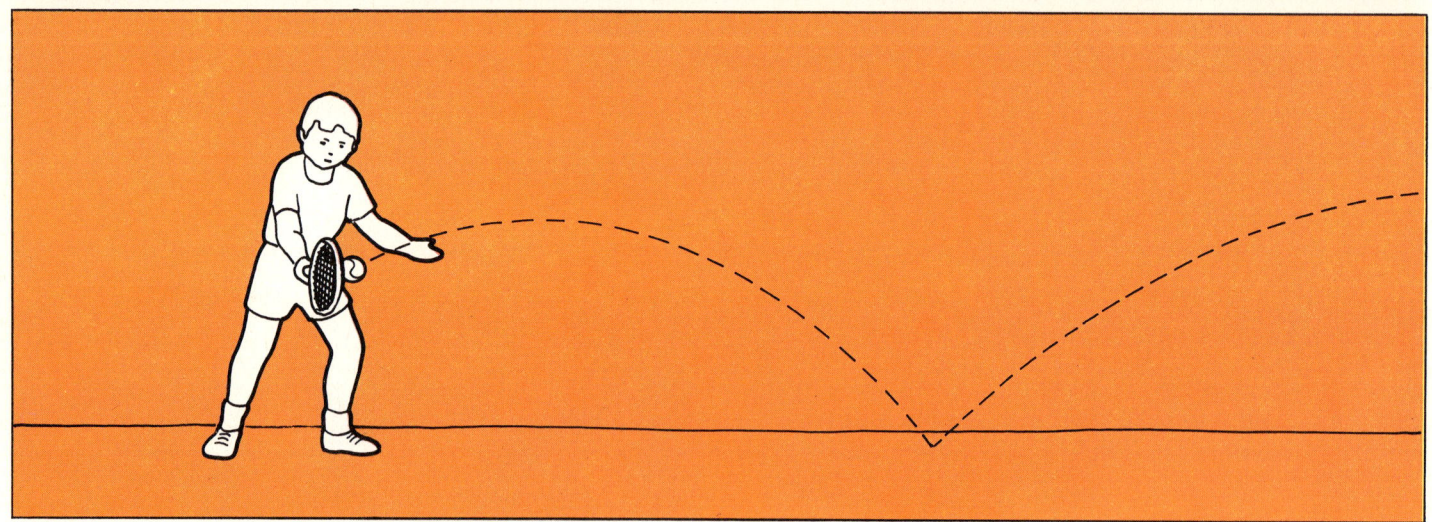

▲ With a partner, practise catching the ball after one bounce, in the easiest position – between the knee and waist height – as it falls from the top of the bounce. Having mastered this, use your racket to hit the dropping ball in the same way

We have all met the natural ball-player. We were probably consistently outplayed in every game at school by someone who was lucky enough to have a natural ability to hit or kick a moving ball. Most of us have to practise to acquire this art, and there are a number of exercises (see page 18) which will help to train our eyes and hands and to co-ordinate our movements.

The first rule in hitting a tennis ball is to keep your eye on it. However, being able to hit the ball does not necessarily mean that you are doing it in the easiest and best way. Is it easier to catch a ball at ankle, knee, waist, shoulder or head height? Try for yourself and you will discover that it is easiest to catch a ball between knees and waist height; it follows that in tennis

this is generally the best height at which to hit the ball. It is also easier to hit it as it is falling from the top of its bounce rather than when it is rising as this gives you more time to position yourself and to play the shot correctly.

As well as positioning yourself to hit the falling ball between knee and waist height, it is generally better to turn sideways to the direction in which you are going to make the shot, particularly for a backhand stroke.

When starting to use a racket to hit the ball, as shown above and on page 18, check that you are using the right basic action for each stroke, swinging the racket for forehands and backhands, punching at volleys and using a throwing action for services.

▲ A good practice – watch the ball closely while you bounce it on the centre of your racket

▲ A group of children with their coach get the feel of controlling the ball on their rackets

▲ Bouncing the ball continuously on the ground with the racket is another ball sense practice

▲ This young boy has taken his eye off the ball, failed to move his position relative to it – and missed it

Ball sense

▲ This young left-hander has opted to take the ball at the difficult shoulder height. He should have moved back to take the falling ball at the easier hitting height of between his knee and waist. (Right-handers should look at this picture in the mirror)

▲ This time he has not watched and judged the ball on to the strings. The ball has dropped too low and his head is in the air – which is why the ball has gone past the outside edge of his racket! You can see that he is not looking at the ball so cannot expect to hit it

There are a number of practice exercises with the ball, with or without a racket, which will help your ball sense and its application. Ball sense is the ability to hit a moving ball. To apply it you need to move into the correct position to catch a falling ball between waist and knee level.

Ball sense practices

With a partner, throw the ball to each other, letting it bounce once and catching it.

By yourself, throw the ball against a wall and catch it. Give yourself a target to hit on the wall to make it more fun.

Bounce the ball continuously on the racket.

Bounce the ball between racket and ground.

Bounce the ball on the edge of the racket. This is difficult; the best score I know of is 155.

Ball sense application practices

Throw the ball against the wall, let it bounce and move your feet so that you catch the falling ball after the top of its bounce.

Throw the ball to a partner, not quite straight so that you move each other backwards, forwards or sideways, always trying to catch it at the correct height and as the ball is falling.

Get a partner to bounce a ball to you, as shown in the diagram on page 14, and hit it at the correct height as it is falling.

▲ If you have a number of balls, the person coaching can give a beginner a useful practice session, feeding him with easy underarm throws from the net

If you practise ball control in this way, it will help to make the game much easier for you when you play. In fact, this is the best way to go about improving your game at the beginning. You might well in theory make the best backhand stroke in the world but, unless you move correctly to take the ball at the right height, your technique will be wasted.

▲ The author shows his young student where the ball should be hit – about waist high and in the centre of the racket. Success (above right)! The ball is hit at the right height, though not quite in the centre of the strings, so the direction will not be quite true

▼ The left-hander has opted for the double-handed backhand (see page 38) and is hitting the ball at the correct height as it is falling; he is watching it right on to his racket strings. Again, right-handers should hold this picture to the mirror to orient it to themselves

Feeding practices

The learner feeds the ball to himself
▲ He stands with his racket up and ready to swing into the forehand action (see page 22). His other hand is prepared to throw the ball up

▲ He throws the ball high into the air, giving himself time to swing his racket back and for the ball to bounce to a reasonable height and at arm's length away from him

▲ The ball has bounced once and the learner is hitting it just after the top of the bounce, between waist and knee height. He may have had to move his position to do so

Feeding the ball from the same side of the net
▲ The learner stands at half court in the ready position (see page 22), but sideways to the net

▲ The feeder gives the ball plenty of air, throwing it gently and quite high; the learner is swinging his racket up and back in a C-shape action to get a good swing at the ball

▲ The ball has bounced once and the learner is hitting it as it is falling and at a reasonable hitting height, watching it on to the racket and aiming to hit it over the net

The feeder stands on the far side of the net
▲ He is still feeding by hand and stands close to the net to make it easier to place the ball where he wants

▲ The learner stands at the base line, square to the net. The feeder has thrown the ball underarm, aiming it high to give the learner time to turn sideways and swing the racket

▲ The learner has moved into position and is hitting the ball correctly. The feeder can vary his throws to make the learner move around a little to get to the ball

The ball is fed by racket

▲ At this early stage it is better to feed from the back of the court if you can do this well, to give the learner time to get into the correct position

▲ Feed with a forehand rather than a serve (the exercise is good for the feeder's own strokes). The learner is getting into position and beginning his swing of the racket

▲ The learner has concentrated on his swing but has forgotten his feet. He is hitting the ball off the wrong leg and will find himself off-balance with little force in his shot

The learner progresses to a rally

▲ The feeder should concentrate on feeding one particular shot that the learner needs to practise – in this case the forehand

▲ If the learner is a better player than the feeder it may be better for the feeder to throw balls in turn from a basket rather than to attempt to rally, as here

▲ Although it is satisfying to keep the ball in play for as long as possible, the learner should concentrate on technique and the feeder watch out for bad habits

The final progression – a match

▲ This is what the learner has been practising his shots for, and so it is important to put some match play into each session

▲ If one player is much the stronger, play to a handicap, with the strong player starting each game minus a point, perhaps, and the weak one plus a point

▲ Alternatively, the stronger player could have only one serve, or be restricted to volleying or use the doubles court his side, to keep up the interest of both players

The forehand

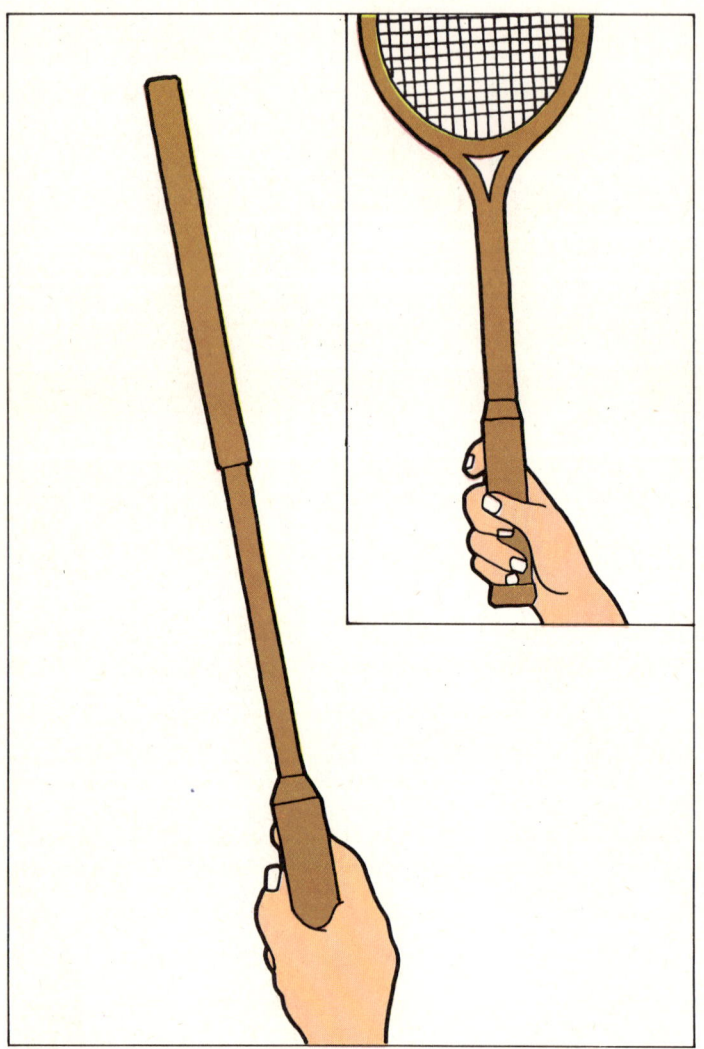

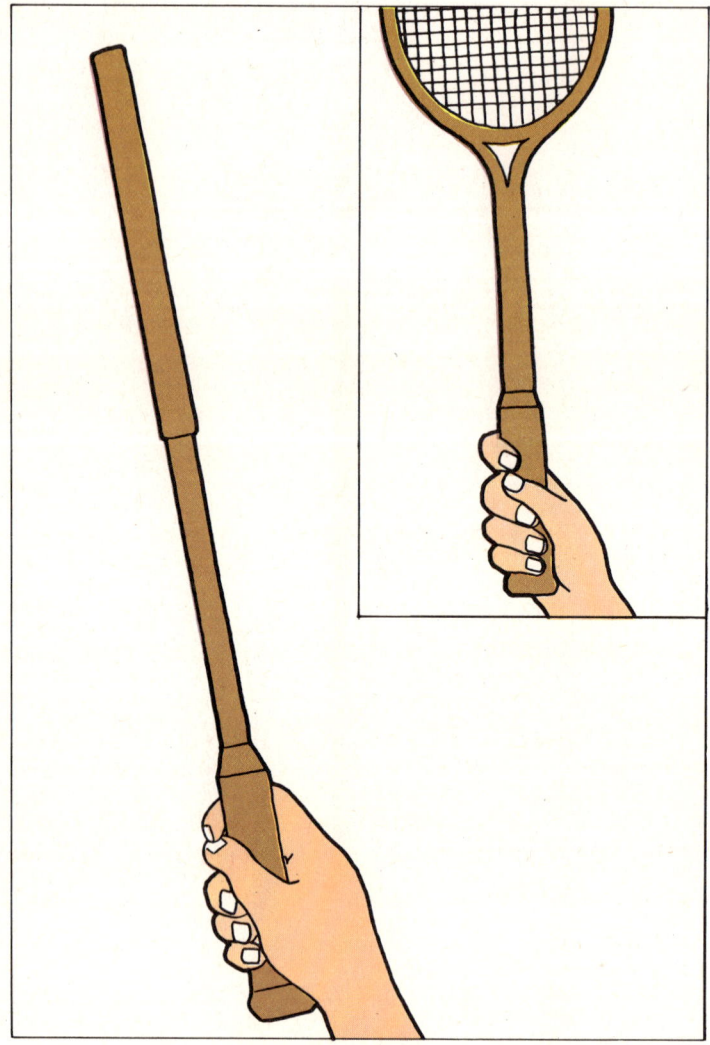

▲ The natural forehand grip is the shake-hands or eastern grip. You literally shake hands with the racket, and the gap in between the thumb and index finger is in line with the head of the racket. The index finger is curled round the handle, to give better control of the racket

▲ In the western grip the gap between the thumb and index finger is further round the back of the racket. The benefit is that the grip makes it easier to play topspin, but the hand has to move in the reverse direction to change grip for volley or backhand

This is the shot that comes most naturally and you may well be inclined not to spend much time practising it.

However, one of the best ways of winning matches is to play within your capabilities, so you should make maximum use of the shots you have at your disposal. Given the opportunity, you will probably use the forehand drive as often as possible, and so you should practise to perfect it.

The word to remember when playing either the forehand drive or the backhand drive is *swing*. Ideally, to put your opponent under pressure, you should hit the ball at a reasonable height over the net and as far to the back of the court as possible. As the court is 23·77m (78ft) long, you will need to give the racket a full swing to achieve this length.

It is also important to try always to keep the racket head above the wrist – 'a cocked wrist' – so that the wrist remains firm during the stroke and does not give way to produce a weak shot.

The grip Shake hands firmly with the racket, bringing the V between the thumb and index finger in line with the head of the racket as shown in the diagrams on the left above; spread or curl the index finger up and round the racket. Initially, this finger will feel superfluous, but eventually, when you have played for a few hours, it will help you to control the wide balls you are having to stretch for and, as an added bonus, help to stop you from suffering from 'tennis elbow'. This is called the eastern grip. There is also the western grip with which a

▲ The player has moved back to hit the ball at waist height, his feet nicely balanced and his weight being transferred to his front foot as he hits the ball through, though his racket head is a little low and it is possible that the ball may not clear the net

young man by the name of Bjorn Borg has achieved a good deal of success! This grip goes further round the back of the racket and makes it easier to impart topspin (see page 24). It is, however, harder to change this grip for backhands and volleys.

I recommend the eastern grip for you to start with but accept that you may prefer the western. If Bjorn Borg can use it, why shouldn't you? But in this book I am assuming that you are adopting the more usual eastern grip.

A young learner is shown the correct ready position ▶

The flat forehand

The player receiving the ball should stand square to the net, in the correct ready position

The racket should be taken back in an upward direction to achieve a smooth C-shaped swing

The player should not turn sideways until he knows that the ball is coming to his forehand

Do not let the racket head drop as it is taken back

▲ The player stands poised in the ready position, knees slightly bent, a firm forehand grip on the racket and the left hand holding the shaft so that the grip can be changed for a backhand if necessary. His weight is on the balls of his feet

▲ He has judged that the ball is coming on to his forehand and is starting to move into the correct position to return the ball by turning his body and feet sideways to it, knees slightly bent

▲ He is taking his racket upwards and backwards in a loop so that he can maintain a free flowing swing even if the ball has spin and bounces unexpectedly. His weight is being transferred to his back (right) foot

Having sorted out your grip, imagine that you are now waiting for your opponent's service and standing about ½-1m (2-3ft) behind the base line in the ready position: you have your knees bent and your weight on the balls of your feet.

Your opponent serves to the forehand. Move quickly into position to take the ball in the easiest hitting position (between knee and waist height and opposite your front knee). Take your racket back in a C shape or looped action, as shown in the third diagram above, which will enable you to play a smooth stroke at any reasonable ball height.

As you take the racket back, turn sideways so that your weight is now balanced on the back foot. Hit the ball at arm's length with a firm wrist (which means that your racket head must be slightly above your wrist), transferring the weight forward on to the leading foot as you do so, in order to put your body weight into the shot at the point of impact. The racket follow-through should chase the ball as far as possible so as to control it on the strings for the longest time. The racket head should finish over your left shoulder, arm still straight, and your left knee should be bent as it takes the weight.

Keep your eye on the ball throughout the stroke, watching it right on to your racket strings. Taking your eye off it is the most common cause of a mis-hit.

The importance of the follow-through cannot be emphasized enough, for if your wrist is not kept firm throughout it but bends at the point of impact, the racket head will finish at about waist level and the ball will stutter into the bottom of the net!

It the racket head finishes at waist height or below the ball will probably go into the net

▲ He has prepared early for his forehand drive, thus allowing himself time to take the racket right back, which will give him more power. His weight is on his back foot

▲ The player is hitting the ball at arm's length and waist height, at the same time stepping forward and transferring his weight to his leading foot to bring his body weight into the shot. Wrist and grip are kept firm

▲ The racket has followed smoothly through and is finishing just above the shoulder, still at arm's length. The racket strings have stayed in contact with the ball as long as possible, giving control. The left (forward) knee is bent

▲ A good early preparation for a forehand, with the racket face taken right back and the player superbly balanced and positioned, her weight on the back foot

▲ She has stepped in to hit the ball at the correct height, although her front leg should be bent to allow the racket head to be above the waist rather than at knee level

▲ A good follow-through: the ball has been hit through with a firm wrist and the player's weight is now established on her leading foot, while she is still in perfect balance

23

The topspin forehand

The front foot should be slightly forward

The feet should not be square to the net, as this will make it difficult to play the correct shot

▲ The player is in the ready position, to which he should return after playing each shot. The knees could be slightly more bent so that he is ready to pounce on any shot his opponent plays

▲ The racket is being taken high up and back in the same way as for a flat forehand, as the player turns sideways, weight transferring to the back foot, in preparation for his shot

▲ Taking the racket back early has given the player a full back swing; left arm and correct footwork give him a good balance and he is now in a good position to play his forehand drive. He is watching the ball closely

Most of the leading players impart some degree of topspin to their shots. A ball spun through the air takes a different path from one without any spin. Spin gives additional control and makes the flight of the ball rise then dip. When the ball hits the court the topspin causes it to gain pace off the court and bounce higher. This means you can hit the ball higher over the net, giving you a greater margin of error, because the spin will dip the ball into court at the far end. When it lands, the higher bounce (particularly beneficial on a hard court), means that your opponent must

◄ The author is showing the learner how he must take his racket through slightly lower so that he can hit upwards, brushing the back of the ball up at the same time as he hits it forward. This imparts topspin, which makes the ball spin forward while in flight

Don't go down or under the ball or you will slice it or send it into the net

The racket face should not finish across the body or there will be little, if any, topspin on the ball

▲ Here is the first basic difference between playing the flat forehand and this topspin shot: the racket has swung through lower to allow it to brush up the back of the ball

▲ The player is hitting the ball with the racket coming upwards and forward. It is important for him to follow the ball through with his racket in the direction in which he is hitting it, so that the strings control the ball for as long as possible

▲ He has hit through and upwards to obtain the best control with the topspin. The racket has finished high over the left shoulder to obtain the maximum controlled topspin on his drive to the far end of the court

either risk taking the ball on the rise or move further back behind the base line, thus giving you more time to judge where the return is coming.

Because the ball dips in flight, the topspin forehand is the basic return of service to the server moving in to the net, as you can direct the ball to his feet and force him to play the difficult half-volley. It is also more difficult for a volleying opponent to judge the flight through the air of the ball with topspin and to hit a crisp volley off it.

To get topspin on a ball, take the racket back in the normal manner for a forehand but swing it through lower, so that, on hitting the ball, you brush up the back of it with the strings. Do not take the racket face straight up the back of the ball but make certain that it stays with the ball for as long as possible so that you maintain power and control. Your follow-through should finish up over your left shoulder, as shown above.

▲ Here the author is taking the ball, possibly a little too low, but you can see that the racket is about to brush upwards and spin the ball. He is well balanced after finishing the shot, (above right), with the racket face, having hit right through, over his shoulder

The sliced forehand

Take the racket up and
back so that the swing is
smooth and continuous

Do not drop the racket to
take it back or you will
have to stop in mid-swing
to bring it forward again,
losing momentum

▲ The player is standing in the ready position, square to the net, weight on the balls of her feet, firm forehand grip on the racket with her other hand on the shaft, ready to change the grip should the ball come on her backhand

▲ The ball is coming on her forehand. She is moving into position to get sideways to the ball and taking the racket up and back early

▲ Having judged where the ball is going to land, the player is well balanced to hit the ball when it falls to between knee and waist height. Weight is on the back foot, eyes on the ball. The high back swing will give power to the shot

Slice (or underspin) takes the speed from a ball, gives it a flat, straight flight and a retarded bounce. To play the sliced forehand, take the racket back in the normal looped action but come through *underneath* the ball, hitting it with the racket face 'open' (slightly tilted to the flight of the ball). Hit through, keeping the wrist firm and the racket face open.

A low-bouncing ball is easier to control with slice. A slice is a good shot to use when approaching the net or for variety of shot or when under pressure from a deep ball.

The drawbacks are that there is less margin for error over the net and in length; and its straight flight makes it easy for the opponent to judge where it will bounce.

◀ The player has moved well back behind the base line to take a high-bouncing ball. He has decided to slice his return, which will give him more control off the high bounce. The racket face is already open – tilted at an angle to the ball

This is the correct position of the racket face: open, so that the ball spins backwards in its flight

If the racket face is kept flat, the ball will not spin

▲ As she swings the racket face through to hit the ball, her wrist is laid back so that the racket is tilted in an open position

▲ This is how the racket face should be on impact with the ball: the firm wrist is tilted back to make the racket face open and spin the ball through the air so that it skids on landing. Her weight is transferring to her leading foot as she hits the ball

▲ She is making a high follow-through so that the ball has remained in contact with the strings as long as possible. The firm wrist means that the racket face has remained open right from impact to the finish of the stroke

▲ The player is under pressure as the ball has dropped very low; on a low ball like this it can be easier to play a sliced return. He is starting to bend right down so that he can control it and he is slightly angling his racket head for the slice

▲ The finish of his stroke. The racket face is still open. Note how low he has bent himself, so that he is able to maintain a firm wrist on impact with the ball. Despite the pressure, he is still well balanced and will soon be in the ready position for the next shot

The changing face of tennis

However did they manage to play in all that gear? When clergyman's daughter Maud Watson became Wimbledon's first woman champion in 1884, she wore a dress with a choker collar, long sleeves, skirts that swept the grass – and whalebone corsets! Men played in knickerbockers and long-sleeved shirts. It was a long, slow evolution to the functional nylon of the contemporary scene

▲ *Then:* Maud Watson's winning style 1884 (left), and Herbert Lawford, who invented topspin; in 1887, champion's knickerbocker glory

▲ *Now:* compare with the outfits of the 1978 mixed doubles finalists: King, Ruffels, McMillan, Stove – clothes for men and women are cool, neat and functional

▲ How daring! The transition from knee-length dresses to shorts: culottes for the smart late-1920s club player

Lawn tennis began as a suitable pastime for Victorian vicarage garden parties. When the game reached championship standards at Wimbledon, the rigid ethics of the day still governed the players. No one dared challenge convention, although it was soon shown that standards of play could be vastly improved by less cumbersome clothing.

In 1887 a 15-year-old girl from Cheshire entered – Lottie Dod. Because of her age, she was permitted to wear a short skirt. Freedom of movement triumphed and Lottie became the youngest-ever Wimbledon champion. She had skill, of course, and she won the title four more times, with ankle-length hemlines when 21!

For men, fashions changed gradually and with little furore. White cricket flannels and shirts soon replaced knickerbockers and, with or without a white cloth cap, remained the uniform until shorts appeared in the 1930s.

Women's fashions hardly changed for years. When Dorothea Lambert Chambers won the singles in 1914 she wore a white ankle-length dress with tucked-in waist. At least the obligatory

continued on page 30

▲ Real (or Royal) Tennis is an indoor game; various outdoor versions gradually evolved into Lawn Tennis

▼ *Then:* patent strung rackets, shaped for Real Tennis; rubber balls, flannel covered

▼ *Now:* streamlined rackets, wood or metal; chemically inflated balls covered with wool and nylon

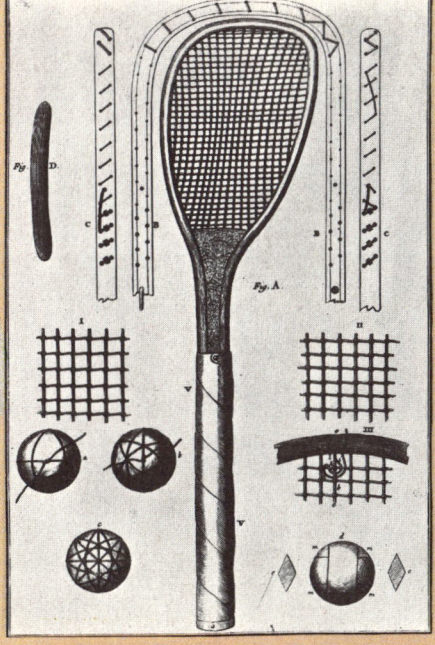

▲ Anyone for tennis? What the well-dressed early 1920s flapper wore

The changing face of tennis

▲ Shorts for stars: Helen Wills Moody, USA (left), eight times champion 1927-38; Bunny Austin (right), Britain's No 2 in the 1930s

▼ A twirl and a stylish swish of lace from Lea Pericoli in 1950 after the 'Gorgeous' Gussie Moran revolution

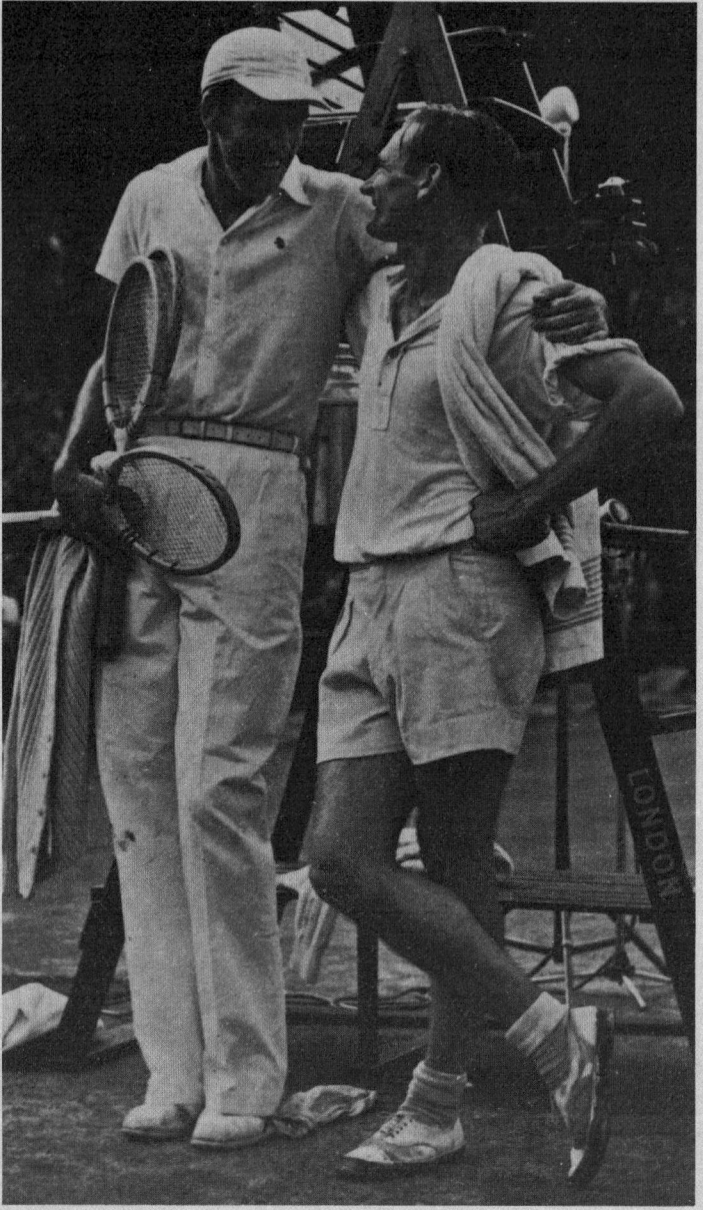

▲ Long and short in the 1946 final: French giant Yves Petra defeated Australian Geoff Brown in five sets

continued from page 28

straw hat had been abandoned. By the time she defended her title again, in 1919 against the supreme Suzanne Lenglen, fashion *had* changed. Lenglen wore a dress to just below her knees, with no sleeves and a low neckline. She still wore long white stockings, however, and it was not until the end of the 1920s that stockings were discarded and hemlines rose above knee level.

Inevitably, shorts – long by today's standards – followed and if they scandalized some, the shock was nothing compared to that produced in 1949 by 'Gorgeous' Gussie Moran's famous frilly panties. Today tennis fashion is functional, simple, and comfortable.

Three great British champions in action. Above, Herbert Lawford and Willie Renshaw in 1881. Renshaw won and went on to defeat the Rev John Hartley in the challenge round for the first of his six successive titles. Lawford finally won in 1887 when Renshaw did not defend. Fred Perry, right, won three Wimbledon titles: in 1934, 1935 and 1936. He missed the Grand Slam in 1934 by losing in France, but won the French title the following year to be first holder of all four titles. Perry was probably the only British player to develop the 'killer' instinct that stamps the champion. He was US champion in 1933, 1934 and 1936; Australian in 1934; and French in 1935

The backhand

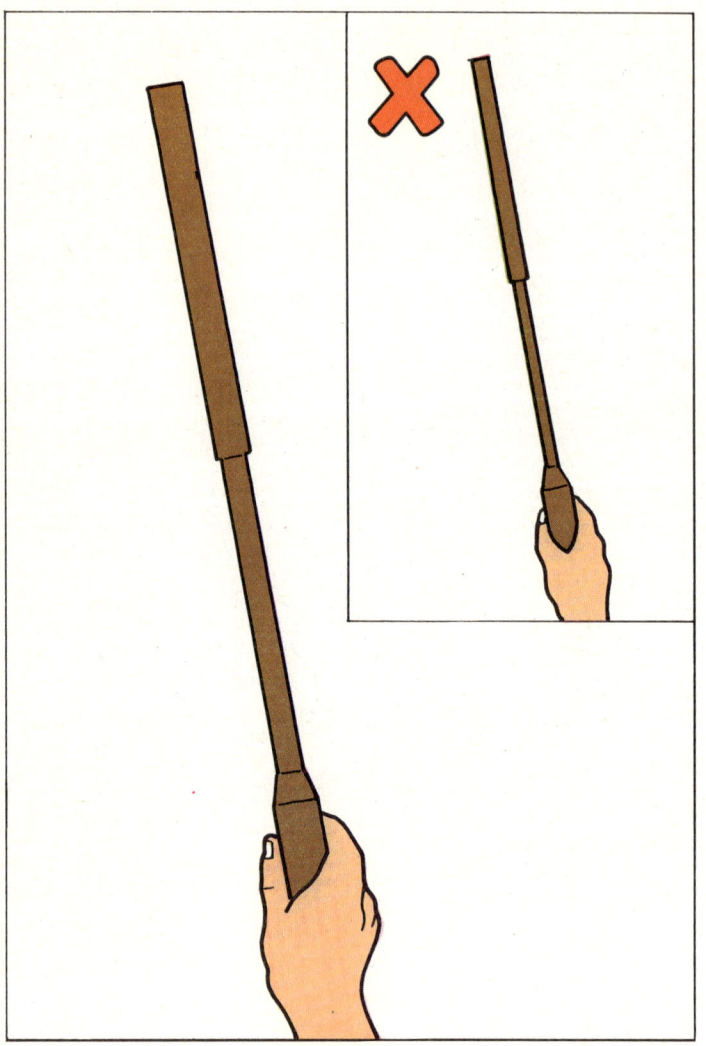

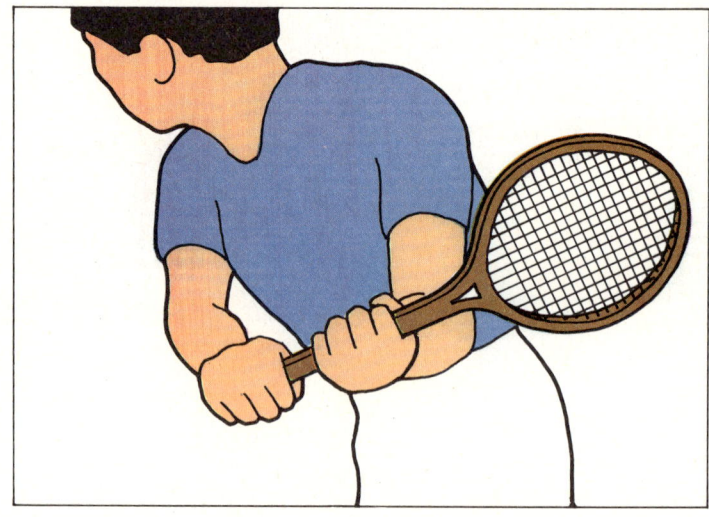

▲ The backhand grip. Inset is the shake-hands forehand grip from which you must change for a backhand, so turn the hand inwards with the thumb at a slightly oblique angle across the back of the handle. The fleshy part below the thumb tucks in behind the handle

▲ The player stands ready with the forehand grip. If he is to play a backhand, he changes grip but keeps his left hand on the handle while he takes his racket behind him; he releases his left hand only when he starts to swing the racket forward at the ball

When you first play tennis the backhand will almost certainly be your weaker side. Many of the top players, such as Ken Rosewall, Jimmy Connors and John Lloyd, have stronger backhands than forehands, perhaps because they, too, were weaker on this side to begin with, so they spent a great deal of time practising their weaker shot. Another reason may be that, once your feet are in the right position, the correct stroke flows naturally.

The grip Hold the racket with the conventional eastern forehand grip (see page 20). Turn your hand inwards a quarter turn on the handle so that the fleshy part below the thumb is tucked in comfortably behind the handle and the thumb itself is across the back of the handle

diagonally – not straight, as this would not allow flexibility of stroke. Your index finger should be curled round the handle to give more control when you have to stretch for a ball.

The stroke Start from the ready position, with the forehand grip and the left hand holding the racket shaft. As soon as you have identified the flight of the ball and decided to hit a backhand, change to the backhand grip, keeping your left hand on the handle, and at the same time take the racket back with both hands. The racket should be taken right back behind you and you will automatically have to move your body from its position square to the net to sideways, with your weight on your back (left) foot and your shoulders turned from the net.

The flat backhand

▲ The player is preparing for the backhand nice and early, allowing himself time for a full swing-through of the racket. His racket is behind him and his weight is on his back foot. He is watching the ball right on to the strings. His shoulder points in the direction of his shot

▲ He has hit the ball through and it is just leaving his racket. His weight has been transferred to his leading foot as it comes forward and he has bent his knees so that he can lift the ball over the net. Compare his position with that in the previous picture

Keep your left hand on the shaft until you swing the racket through hitting the falling ball between knee and waist height, as reasonably far away from you as possible, and when it is level with your front foot. As you hit the ball, transfer your weight to your front foot, bending the knee. Follow the ball right through, making sure the racket face follows as far as it can in the direction in which you have hit the ball, thus giving control. The racket follow-through should finish at approximately shoulder height. The wrist should remain firm throughout the stroke.

This is far too complicated to digest all at once, so think initially of two words while playing a backhand: 'swing' and 'lift'. Practise shadow swings, telling yourself to *swing* the racket and *lift* the ball over the net. Next, concentrating on

one of these points at a time, gradually put them all into your stroke: early preparation; taking the racket back and changing the grip; swinging through with knees bent; hitting the falling ball at the right height and distance; following through with the racket to shoulder height. Keep the wrist firm throughout.

These precepts will help you to play a smooth backhand even when your opponent puts you under pressure.

The sliced backhand

 Stand with both hands on the racket so that the grip can be changed if the ball is on the backhand

For a backhand it is important to be sideways to the net and have both knees bent

 If you hold your racket with one hand, it will be impossible to change grips for a backhand

Do not stand square to the ball nor keep your legs straight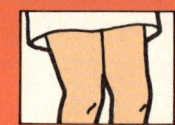

▲ The player is standing poised in the ready position, using the forehand grip, but with the left hand holding the shaft ready to change the grip if the ball comes to her backhand

▲ The ball is on her backhand. She changes her grip as she takes the racket back with both hands, putting her in the important sideways position, weight on her back foot

▲ She has taken the racket right back so that it can be seen on the other side of her body. The left hand is still on the racket, bringing her leading shoulder into the correct position. Both her knees are bent

The sliced backhand is most players' normal backhand shot; top players are able to use slice, flat or topspin – as tactics demand. The sliced backhand is generally used from the back of the court for hitting deep to the other end of the court, and is the usual approach shot when coming in to the net from the back of the court.

To play a sliced backhand, change to the backhand grip (page 32) and with both hands take the racket back behind you to about just under shoulder height, turning yourself sideways and placing your weight on your back foot. As you take the racket back, turn your wrists so that the racket face is open (tilted, playing-face up). Release your left hand and swing through, transferring your weight to your front leg. Keep

The player is hitting the ball at arm's length with his weight coming on to his leading foot; his wrist is cocked and firm, keeping the racket head up and slightly tilted so that the shot is sliced and the ball spins backwards in flight. He is watching it closely ▶

▲ Letting go with the left hand, she swings her racket through, keeping the face open (tilted, face up) and up, and her wrist firm. Her weight is coming forward with the swing

▲ She is hitting the ball with the racket face still open, imparting slice and making the ball spin backwards which gives her more control. Her weight is now on her front foot, her left arm is helping her balance, and her right arm is straightening

▲ She has followed through high, keeping the ball on the racket strings as long as possible. Her wrist has stayed firm, lifting the ball over the net. Knees are bent and the weight is on the leading foot

the racket face open so that the ball will be spinning backwards as it leaves the racket. Keep your wrist firm and both knees bent throughout. Finish with the racket face still open and high over your shoulder, your arm fully stretched out. Keep your head down as you watch the ball hit the racket; if you lift your head too early, the ball will probably sail high out of court.

The benefits of the backhand slice are that it is easier to control the ball than with a flat stroke, and, on a low-bouncing court (such as grass or wood), the ball does not rise very much.

The disadvantages are that the flight of the ball is predictable, and, on a hard court, the ball grips the surface on bouncing and slows down, giving your opponent more time for his shot.

◄ He is now hitting through the shot and chasing the ball with his racket face, so that they remain in contact as long as possible. Note the stretched hitting arm, the balancing left arm and the bent right knee. The follow-through will continue slightly upwards

The topspin backhand

Keep both hands on the racket while you wait to see on which side the ball is coming

Your knees should be bent so that you can lift the ball over the net

Your left hand should not be taken from the racket until the back swing is completed and the forward one is started

Your legs should not be straight or close together and you should not stand square to the net

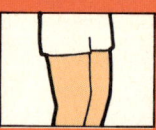

▲ To hit a topspin backhand, the player has changed to his usual backhand grip and with both hands is taking the racket back slightly lower than he would for a flat or sliced backhand. Weight is being transferred to his back foot

▲ He has taken the racket head right back behind him, still with both hands so that his leading shoulder is automatically in the right position and he is sideways to the net. He is watching the ball closely

▲ He is starting to swing forward and letting go with his left hand. Both knees are bent. The racket head is still comparatively low

This shot is much more difficult to perfect than a sliced backhand, but it is a very important shot if you wish to reach a reasonably high standard in the game.

To play the shot, take the racket back quite low with both hands, with the racket swing-through starting from below knee height. When the racket face connects with the ball, it should be flat and should brush up the back of the ball to a follow-through above head height. Again, it is very important that the knees are bent, the wrist is firm and the head stays down for as long as possible, or the ball will travel too high and may go out of court.

The considerable benefit of topspin is that the flight of the ball changes as it travels, first rising

In the first picture, the player has moved into position and is well balanced. His racket is starting to come through to brush up the back of the ball to make it spin. In the second picture, he is finishing his follow-through with the high flourish necessary for a good deal of spin ▶

▲ He hits at about knee height, with a firm wrist, bent knees and the racket face flat as it starts to move up the back of the ball, causing it to spin forward as it flies through the air

▲ The racket face is starting to follow-through, chasing the ball in the direction in which it has been hit and moving upwards on a firm wrist. Weight is on the right foot

▲ The follow-through is high because the racket head has moved upwards to impart a strong topspin, which will make the flight of the ball rise then dip on the other side of the net. It will be difficult for the opponent to judge and the high bounce will drive him back

and then dipping to land. This makes the shot difficult for your opponent to judge, and so most leading players play topspin to a volleying opponent to make the ball dip to his feet. The ball gathers pace on hitting the ground and bounces high. This means that your ground strokes (those played off the bounce) become more aggressive, gaining power off the court; a lot of topspin gives a high bounce which will make your opponent retreat and find it difficult to play a good return.

The basic problem with the topspin backhand is that most players find it more difficult to play with any degree of control unless they play a great deal of tennis, but it well repays time spent practising it.

The player really has only one racket! (She has beaten the shutter speed of the camera.) She is finishing a topspin backhand with her racket at arm's length in a classic follow-through. Note the position of her front foot, sideways to the shot, and her excellent balance ▶

The double-handed backhand

Turn your right shoulder to the net as you prepare to make the stroke

Don't stay facing the net or your stroke will be cramped and difficult to send where you want it

▲ The double-handed backhander waits for the ball in the normal ready position, with the forehand grip and both hands on the racket

▲ Like the single-hander, he changes his grip as he turns sideways to the ball. Even if you start double-handed, you may well change to playing single-handed later, so it is a good idea to get into the habit of changing grips

▲ He swings the racket right back, with his left hand as close as possible on the handle to his right one so that he gains as much reach as he can. His weight is going on to his back foot

Up until ten years ago many official lawn tennis organizations recommended that a learner with a double-handed backhand should be taught to play the stroke single-handed. Today this is hardly valid with the superb results achieved by many double-handers – Borg, Connors, Chris Lloyd, Tracy Austin – and they seem to find it easy to make a last-second adjustment to the direction in which they hit the ball, to the confusion of their opponents.

Juniors now start to learn to play tennis at a tender age when their arms and wrists have little strength. In order to keep the racket head up they need to use two hands, but may later want to change to one.

There are variations in the actual grip used by leading two-handed players. Many of them don't change from their normal forehand grip, just adding their left hand immediately above the right with the V between finger and thumb in line with the racket head. I suggest beginners

change to the normal backhand grip for a double-handed backhand, and add the other hand as above, so that eventually they can play single-handed. The disadvantage of using two hands is that your reach is restricted and so you have to be exceptionally quick on your feet.

To play the shot, grip the racket firmly, hands close together, take the racket back reasonably low then swing through, brushing up the back of the ball to give it a certain amount of topspin (the topspin is the most natural one for a double-hander) and follow-through with the full swing.

The player has moved into position for her double-handed backhand in good time, her racket swept back and her weight on her back foot. She swings through (lower picture), knees bent low and head over the ball, then finishes (far right) with her weight over her leading foot ▶

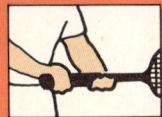

▲ He starts his swing-through, keeping the racket head cocked above his wrists, and transferring his weight forward as he swings into the ball

▲ The player is hitting the ball with topspin – the natural shot for a double-hander. The racket face is flat and starting to brush up the back of the ball to give it spin

▲ He is following all the way through with his racket. Some double-handers, such as Borg, tend to take their left hand off the racket at the end of the follow-through. If you find this happens, I suggest you start to play a normal one-handed stroke

Stroke practice

It is important that, as well as playing matches, you practise your strokes. When playing with someone as keen to progress as yourself, it is more beneficial to split an hour and a half's play into, say, half an hour's stroke practice then an hour's match play.

The first basic practice is to have balls thrown to you underarm (see page 18). The feeder should throw them first on one spot, then on different ones to encourage you to move around. A basketful of balls from a hand feeder can give you a hard three or four minutes' work-out. To make the practice more skilful, put targets on the court at which to aim your strokes.

For consistency, practice in pairs with a long rally, counting the number of strokes that you can make consecutively.

To practise length, rally in between the service and base lines, not counting shots that land short.

Playing against two opponents can put you under pressure and make you react quickly. Your two opponents should play from the back of the court and use a lot of balls to pressurize you.

Whether feeding or returning, always concentrate on playing your shots with the correct technique, or you may unconsciously acquire bad habits.

▲ All the basic shots – services, forehands, backhands and volleys – can be practised on your own, hitting against a wall. Emphasis should be placed on controlling the ball rather than trying to knock the cover off it, and on concentrating on achieving a good technique on each shot.

▼ Below and left, two players are pressurizing one. The two feeders are volleying and the single player is hitting ground strokes. There are many similar practices: feeders at the back and the single player at the net; all players at the back, giving the single player a specific part of the court at which to aim, and so on

▲ Far left, the learner learns to control the ball across court to the feeder, who is throwing to his forehand; then they repeat the exercise with his backhand. Finally, the learner stands at the middle of the service line so that he has to move around to get into position to hit a forehand or a backhand, whichever is fed to him

Approach shots

The wrist should be kept firm and cocked throughout the shot

Do not let the racket head drop but bend your knees to get it low enough

The forehand approach shot

▲ The player has judged her opponent's ball to be landing short, at around mid-court. She has taken her racket back early as she moves to the ball to play a sliced forehand deep into her opponent's court

▲ The ball has a low bounce and she is compensating by bending low. She is keeping her wrist firm and hitting with the racket face open to give the ball slice, so that it skids low on landing. Her knees are bent and her weight is coming forward

▲ The follow-through is not quite as high as for a flat forehand. Her weight is on her leading foot and helps her move quickly to the net to intercept the next return

Do not drop the racket head, nor close the face for a flat shot, or the ball will go into the net

The backhand approach shot

▲ The player has judged the ball is going to land in mid-court and has decided to go in to the net. She has run to meet it and is taking her racket back as she moves into position

▲ The player is well balanced and is hitting the ball as it rises on its bounce, to give her opponent less time to move into position and herself more time to get an extra couple of paces closer to the net

▲ She has kept the racket face open to put slice on the ball and is following-through only high enough to lift the ball over the net. Both knees are bent and the weight is on her right foot, which will give impetus to her sprint to the net

A shot deep to the back of the court as you run in to the net will give you time to get into a good position to volley the return. Wait for the right opening – a weak return from your opponent that lands short. You should then move quickly into position for the shot, if possible taking the ball early as it rises from the bounce. This gives your opponent less time to move back for your deep drive. Hit the ball with a firm wrist and the racket face open to control the shot with slice, which will make the ball skid low when it bounces, causing your opponent to hit the ball upwards. By then you should be at the net ready to punch away a volley for a winner.

Errors are caused by choosing the wrong ball for the approach or by trying from mid-court to hit a risky big winner when it would be safer to get the ball back deep, hoping to volley a winner off the next shot from the net.

In the photographs, the player has just hit good forehand and backhand approach shots.

Portrait of a superstar

Superstars are the aces in the tennis pack. The superstar will fly about 250,000 miles to win more than $500,000 in a year. He will jet to Australia and the Far East; to Rome, Paris, Berlin, London; he will flit east, west and mid-USA, go north to Canada and south to Buenos Aires. His life at the top will last, on average, six years. The superstar astride the tennis world today is Bjorn Borg of Sweden. He achieved his first successes in his teens and looks set for a long reign

At Boca, West Florida, USA, Bjorn Borg played 95 minutes of devastating tennis and blasted one of his greatest rivals, American Jimmy Connors, 6-2, 6-3. That victory was sweeter to the 22-year-old superstar than the record $150,000 prize he picked up.

Borg made his Wimbledon debut when he was a lad of 17 in 1973 – a bad year when top professionals nearly wrecked the meeting by a last-minute walk-out. But young Borg emerged as one of the saviours of the tournament. He gathered a vocal young fan club and reached the quarter-finals. In 1974 he won the Italian and French singles but, alas, went out tamely in round three at Wimbledon. Connors won that year. In 1975, Borg again came to Wimbledon as French champion; this time the eventual winner, Arthur Ashe, eliminated him in the quarter-finals.

When Borg came back in 1976 he was World Championship Tennis champion, having won that title at Dallas, Texas, while still a teenager. He showed what world championship form meant when he sailed through Wimbledon without losing a set, to defeat Ilie Nastase in the final. After that came the Wimbledon run that lifted him into the superstar class.

He was only 22 when he equalled Fred Perry's 42-year-old record of three Wimbledon singles titles in a row – truly, a superstar performance – then he went on to make it five successive championships, in 1980 playing against his great rival, John McEnroe. When McEnroe conquered Borg in the World Championship Tennis finals at Dallas in 1979 he said Borg was still the world's greatest player; and he certainly seems set to stay the superstar course.

Polished and powerful, Bjorn Borg, in full flight on the forehand and (inset) holding the Wimbledon trophy

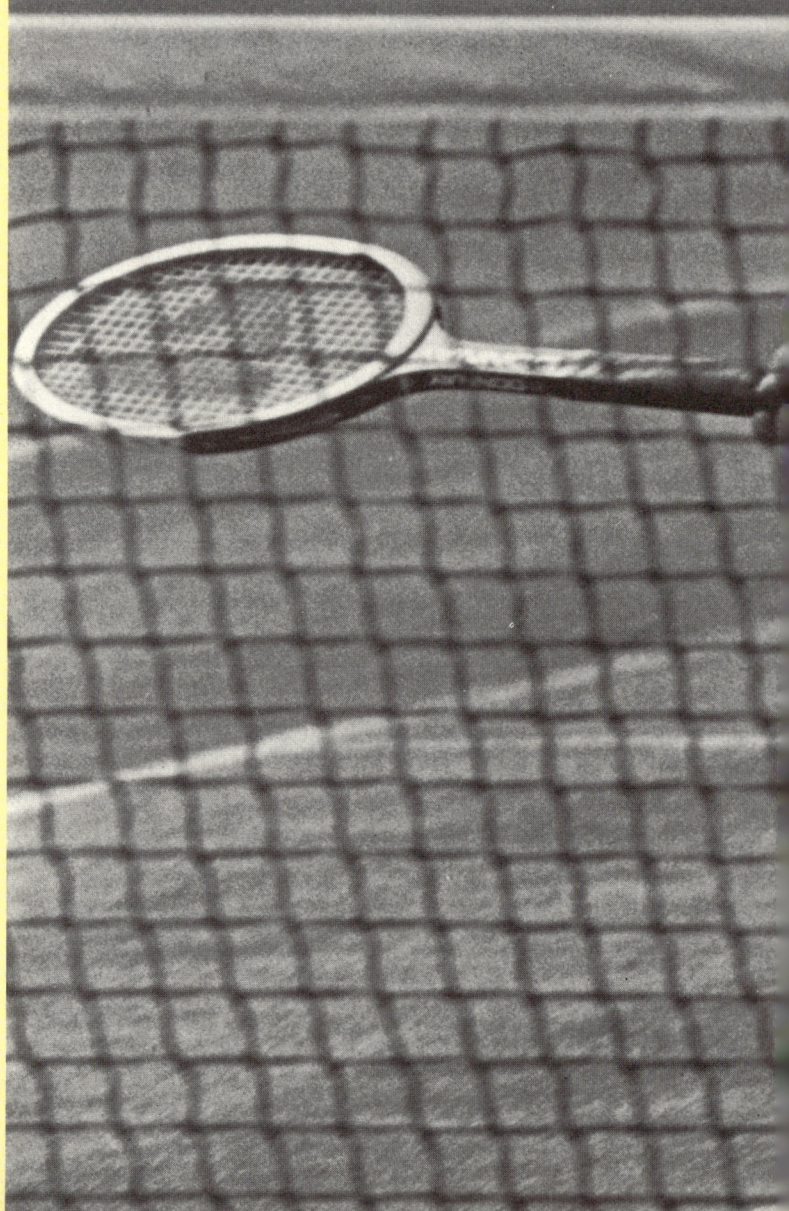

The service

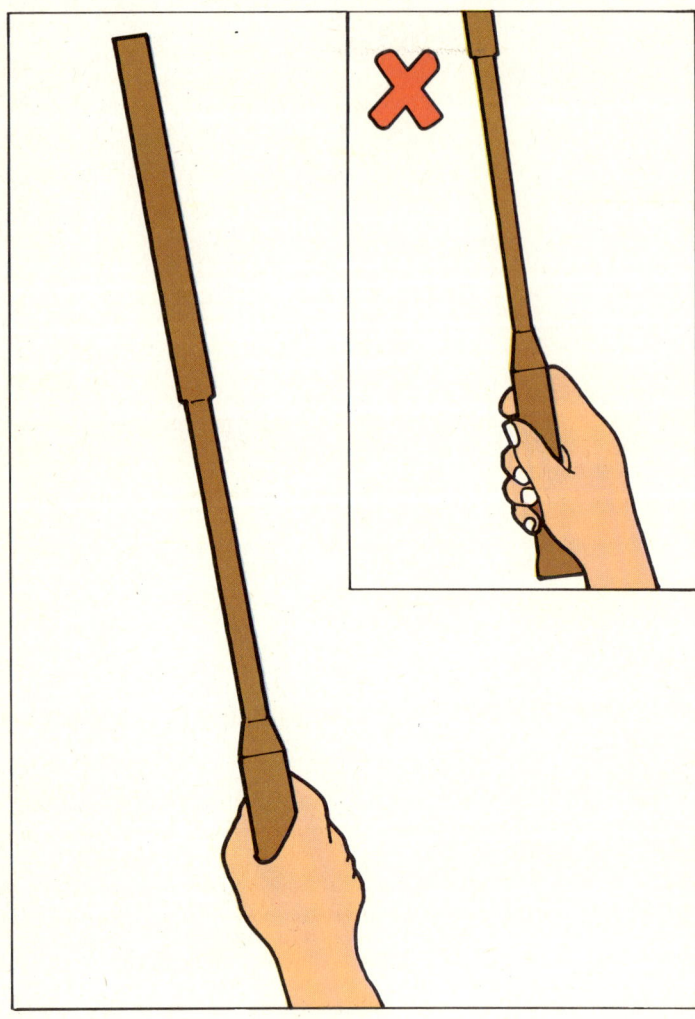

▲ The correct 'chopper' service grip. The gap between thumb and index finger should be in line with the inside edge of the racket shaft. This grip allows you to deliver any type of service, whereas the inset 'frying-pan' grip is wrong as it allows only a flat service to be hit

The service can be a match winner or just the opposite. If you watch the tennis stars, you will find they seem capable of winning service game after service game. It is exceedingly difficult on fast grass to return Roscoe Tanner's 140 mph service with any degree of accuracy!

When first you play tennis, it seems to be more difficult to win your own service game than to break your opponent's. At beginner level, if you can hold your service game only once you may well win the set. Start now to remedy this so that you consistently win service.

The grip A beginner is inclined to pick the racket up to serve with the palm of the hand behind it. This 'frying-pan' grip should be discouraged; it does not allow you to angle the racket face to put spin on the ball, and although you can hit your first service quite hard, your safe second is usually a soft patball which your opponent can slaughter.

The better grip is the 'chopper', illustrated on the left. Hold the racket in the eastern forehand grip (see page 20), the V between thumb and index finger in line with the head of the racket, then turn the hand slightly inwards on the handle, so that the ridge of the handle nestles in between thumb and index finger. This will feel very odd at first, but persevere with it.

The service is the only stroke in which you can hold the racket with a relaxed grip rather than a firm one. This gives a pleasant relaxed service, allowing you to use your wrist as well as your arm. It is from the wrist that the best players get their power.

The preparation Take your time to serve. In the photograph on the left, the author is bouncing the ball before serving. Many top players do this to collect and prepare themselves. It gives them time to decide on the type of service to use, the speed and placing of it and whether to move in to the net after it or to stay back.

Start with two balls, either both in your hand or with one in your pocket. There is nothing worse than playing someone who misses his first service, then wanders off to find a ball for his second.

The service action can be likened to a throw; it is useful to practise the action by throwing a ball overarm upwards to the other end of the court.

◄ Bouncing the ball helps to collect and prepare yourself before the service

Jimmy Connors (USA), unorthodox left-hander, hitting a first service and putting everything into it ▶

▲ The serving position is fine – except that the front foot is on the line, causing a foot fault

▲ A good service action but he has stepped into court before hitting the ball – another foot fault

▲ This time he is in the correct position, similar to the first but with both feet behind the line

Service action Place your feet comfortably behind (not on) the base line, left foot pointing at approximately the right net post and left shoulder pointing in the direction in which you want the ball to travel.

Stand with the ball against the racket strings, the racket head opposite your face and your arms stretched out in front but relaxed. This enables you to bring both arms down smoothly together.

Throw the ball up, stretching your arm before releasing it, and at the same time swing the racket down and back as if to scratch your back with it, with a gap of about 15cm (6in) between the racket head and your back.

'Throw' the racket head at the ball. You should hit the ball at the top of your reach and when the ball has dropped about 5-8cm (2-3in). It should be sufficiently far in front of you so that, if it hit the ground, it would land 30-45cm (12-18in) away, enabling you to put your body weight into the stroke. The racket head should finish on the left side of your body, having 'hit the ball through' smoothly and powerfully.

You can break the action down into three parts when practising:
1 Stand ready with the ball against the racket.
2 Place the ball in the air and swing the racket behind you.
3 Throw the racket head at the ball, hitting at arm's length.

Relax while you are serving and do not grip the racket too tightly; have your feet comfortably spaced behind the line as shown in the photograph above.

When you first use the 'chopper' grip, the ball may spin out to the left of the box you are aiming at; to compensate, adjust your wrist position so that the racket face is not so acutely angled to the ball.

Do not try to hit the ball too hard at first; concentrate on correct action and hitting into court. If it is a fault, it is better to have hit the ball out than into the net.

You need neither partner nor wall when practising the service; just take as many balls as you can find on to the nearest court and put your new service into action.

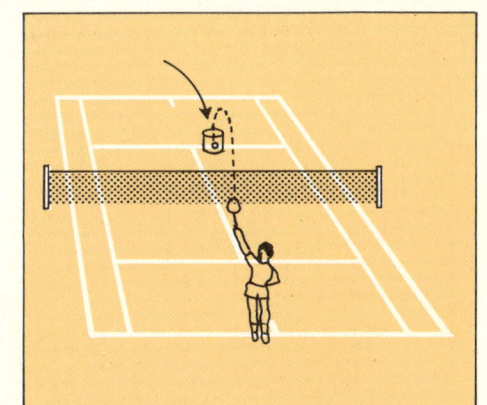 

▲ It is good service practice to put a target on the court and try to hit it. The server has placed her target so that she is serving as near to the centre line as she can, which would be to a right-hander's backhand

The server is placing the target at ▶ each corner of the service box in turn. Never sit around waiting for an opponent to arrive if there is a spare court and balls. If you have no target, you can count the number of times you serve the ball into the correct court

Types of service The ideal combination of service is probably a flattish first service and a topspin second service, with the ability to put in a sliced service when you want to. As this is the only time you dictate totally to your opponent, vary your services so that he does not know what is coming next and put most on his weaker side.

Left-handers If you are left-handed, you have a big advantage when playing a right-hander.

Your sliced service will go to his backhand. If you can put a really 'fizzy' slice on your service, you should be able, when serving to his backhand court, to take him well out of position into (or even outside) the tramlines to receive it. The heavily sliced left-hander's service on a low-bouncing court is one of the most difficult for a right-hander to return. Left-handers are fairly rare, so your service will come from an unaccustomed angle.

The flat service

Always start your swing and put the ball up at the same time, rhythmically

If you don't synchronize movements of racket and ball you will get a jerky effect and little power

At this point, your foot must not stray over the line or it will be a fault

▲ Always start your service in the same relaxed position: ball against the racket, feet comfortably spread, left foot pointing at about the right net post and left shoulder pointing in the direction that you want the ball to go, as shown here

▲ With a relaxed 'chopper' grip, the player has brought the racket and ball down. Without stopping the movement, she is throwing the ball up with stretched arm and, at the same time, sweeping the racket slowly under and back behind her

▲ Her racket is swung behind her as the ball goes up, and her weight is poised on her left foot. She is taking care not to let her leading foot wander on to court at this point – a common cause of a foot fault

▲ When first attempting to serve (left), most of us use the inefficient 'frying-pan' grip, take the racket up forwards, stop, then weakly push the ball. Make sure you use the 'chopper' grip (right), and take the racket under and back to get a smooth powerful throwing action

Players who use a flat first service usually follow with spin on the second. Your flat first service should be really fast but within your capabilities. The better players hit 60 to 80 per cent of their first services into court – what a conservation of energy!

For a flat service, stand sideways behind the service line, with feet comfortably apart, left foot pointing to the right net post. Use the 'chopper' grip. Place the ball up a little in front of you; hit it at full stretch to make the most use of your height, with the racket face hitting the ball full on. Your body should pivot on your left foot, with your right foot and weight coming forward as you hit the ball. You will probably finish up a couple of strides into court but you must not put a foot down over the line before you hit the ball or it will be a fault.

As your tennis improves and you follow the ball to the net, a shot like this will start you on your way to it.

The racket face should be
flat as it hits the ball

Don't take the racket
straight down in the
follow-through or you
will find yourself off
balance

▲ She has dropped the racket head behind her (which her relaxed grip allows), ready for a full swing at the lofted ball

▲ Using her full height, she hits the ball just as it starts to drop from the top of the throw, pivoting on her left foot as she transfers her weight to the right one. The racket face is flat as it hits the ball

▲ Her racket face has followed-through across her body and her weight is fully transferred to her right foot, making it simple to run in to the net if she wishes

▲ The first picture shows the player using her full reach to serve the ball; the second and third show a player using weight and height to good effect. On the right is Arthur Ashe, 1975 Wimbledon champion, his speeding racket head a blur as he serves

The sliced service

The feet should still be behind the base line

The front foot must not move into court before the ball is hit, as this will cause a foot fault

▲ The server stands in the ready position, with the correct 'chopper' grip and the ball held against the racket face. He relaxes, takes his time and decides what type of service to play, where to place the ball and whether to stay back or move in

▲ He places the ball up slightly to the right, fully extending his arm before he releases it. At the same time, he slowly takes his racket back and under. The correct placing of the ball is one of the most important parts of the service action

▲ He is starting to drop the racket head behind him with a relaxed grip as his shoulders turn with the movement. His weight is poised on his left foot

Having decided that your first service will be a fast, flat, attacking one, it is important that your second should be reliable, as well as difficult for your opponent to return.

To ensure a reasonable amount of accuracy, without resorting to a patball, you can put spin on the ball. The easiest spin to put on is slice.

To play a sliced service, place the ball up so that it is a little further back and to the right than for a flat service, and, using the 'chopper' grip, hit the ball with the racket face angled so that the ball brushes across the strings. The racket head can still meet the ball at speed but the ball will keep in contact with the racket for a longer time, giving greater control.

◀ The player is about to serve, racket face and ball together. He is balanced slightly forward, ready to swing back and throw the ball up smoothly; he has decided on the type of service he is going to play, where he is going to put the ball, and whether he will move in to the net or stay back

The racket face should slide round the outside of the ball, to make it spin

If the racket face is flat against the ball there will be no spin

▲ He is beginning to 'throw' the racket face upwards to hit the ball with a forceful but slightly angled and glancing shot as it reaches the top of its path and starts to drop

▲ As the ball has been placed to the right, he slides the racket face round the outside of it to give it spin, his weight coming forward as he does so. His foot must not touch down inside the court until the ball has been hit

▲ His racket face is swung across his body in the follow-through. His weight has gone into the service and he is ready either to run to the net without stopping or to recover and stay at the back of the court

The spin gives the benefit of greater control, perhaps not to begin with but soon if you practise a lot, and its sliding bounce makes it more difficult for your opponent to return.

Disadvantages are that the sliced service does not give you much margin for error in the height at which it travels over the net, and if your opponent is right-handed you are serving to his strength with a ball that bounces to his forehand; when he has judged the speed of the service he can put you under pressure with attacking returns.

If you are playing a left-hander, your sliced service has the advantage of going to his normally weaker backhand.

◀ A static demonstration by the author of the correct hitting position for the sliced service. Note the firm 'chopper' grip on the racket, which has its face slightly slanted to the path the ball is to take so that the ball spins as it leaves the racket. Note, too, the stretched arm

53

The topspin service

Both feet should remain behind the base line until the ball is hit

If the front foot is allowed to slide over the base line before the ball is hit, it is a foot fault

▲ The server is in the normal serving position, with 'chopper' grip and ball held against racket, feet apart behind the line. He is generally relaxed as he plans his service tactic; he has decided on topspin, which will make the ball rise then dip in flight

▲ He throws the ball up for this service a little back over his left shoulder. At the same time, he sweeps his racket down and back

▲ Because the ball is over his left shoulder, he is arching his back as he watches the ball closely

Most of the better players use topspin on their second service after a flat first one; topspin takes the ball higher over the net, giving a greater margin of error, and it kicks to the right off the court to the right-hander's backhand. Women generally find it difficult, but Virginia Wade and Billie Jean King use it with telling effect.

To serve with topspin, place the ball up a little in front of you and to your left, so that if you let it bounce it would land about 15cm (6in) inside the court and 15cm (6in) to the left of your leading foot. This time let the ball drop 12-15cm (5-6in) from the top of the throw up and, arching your body, hit *upwards* across the back of the ball.

◄ The learner gets the feel of the topspin service, the author emphasizing the correct grip and demonstrating how the racket brushes up and across the back of the ball as it is hit forward across the net. Expert coaching like this saves the learner much time and frustration

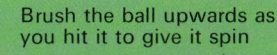

Brush the ball upwards as you hit it to give it spin

▲ As he starts to throw his racket head at the ball, his body is arched right back with his weight on his left foot

▲ His racket face is brushing up the back of the ball at the same time as he hits it forward, giving it spin that will provide extra height over the net, and the server with the extra control needed for a second service

▲ His right foot has come forward to take his weight and the racket head has swept down to his left-hand side, across his body

The racket should finish to the left of your body. Brushing upwards across the back of the ball will cause it to spin higher over the net and dip into court, like a topspin forehand, and on bouncing it will kick to your right, on to your opponent's theoretically weaker backhand.

This service needs a lot of practice before you can use it confidently. If you have a weak back, the arching movement will put strain on it; and you should stick to slice for your second service.

The American kick service This is similar to the topspin except that you place the ball further behind you over your left shoulder, arch your back more, brush up and right across the back of the ball so that your racket face finishes on the right of your body. This gives greater spin and kick on the bounce but the ball travels more slowly and gives a good-class opponent the chance to take the ball early before it has had time to kick very far.

▲ For the American kick service, the player places the ball further over his left shoulder and arches his back more to get extra spin, with the racket this time finishing on the right of his body. Because this action gives him no impetus towards the net, he stays behind the base line

The return of service

This shot is as important as any in the game for, if you do not hit more than half your returns of service back into court, you cannot win your opponent's service, and if you cannot break service you cannot win the match.

In receiving service your first consideration is to get the ball back and your second to do it as well as possible.

Receiving position Stand in the ready position, on your toes, knees bent, firm forehand grip and both hands on the racket. Your position relative to the base line depends on how fast your opponent's service is. For a fast service, you will stand well behind the base line and, for a slow one, inside it. The second service is usually slower than the first, for your opponent must get this one into court, so move in a little. Once you play at a reasonable standard of tennis, you should aim to get the first service back as best you can but the second you should be able to attack.

If your ground strokes are stronger on one side than the other, you should use your strongest stroke when possible, so on your opponent's weaker second service, move into a position from which you can play the return on your stronger side. By moving around like this, you tempt him to go for an attacking second service and he will generally hit a few double faults in trying to put the ball into the gap which is left!

The return If your opponent is serving and staying at the back of the court, your return generally should be a deep one, with an occasional short one to bring him to the net – particularly if he is a weak volleyer – or a wide one to take him out of position into the tramlines. If he is a serve-and-rush-to-the-net player, aim to pass him as he races in, or put a chip shot (short, sliced shot) at his feet, making him play a half-volley (see page 68).

If he has a big, fast service, either block it back by holding your racket firmly with very little back swing or follow-through, or lob him so that he will not be able to race in to kill a weak return from the net. Attack the easier second service with topspin returns.

Whatever your tactics, vary your returns and your receiving position so that your opponent is never quite sure what you are about to do, bearing in mind that your primary aim is to return the ball into court.

▲ Normally you should stand just behind the base line for the first service and inside it for the weaker second. This will vary according to the power of the service

▲ In a match in London's Albert Hall, the player is poised ready to receive any type of service sent to him on either backhand or forehand side

▲ Jimmy Connors takes the ball early with his unique double-handed shot, so that he can move up to the net in its wake and attack his opponent's return

▲ The reply to a super-fast service – block, by holding the racket firmly, with a very short backswing and follow-through, as it needs little power

▲ The service is a short one and the player has attacked it off the top of the bounce with a decisive forehand hit down from above net level

▲ Former Wimbledon champion Stan Smith blocks a very fast service that has come whizzing down the centre line to his backhand

The ladies of the court

Women's tennis is more than a sport. It is a social revolution. The multi-million-dollar commercial enterprise starring the modern super athletes is a world away from the thirteen daring Victorian misses who ended Wimbledon's male dominance in 1884

Women first invaded championship tennis in Ireland in 1879. Wimbledon held out for another five years, but even then it could hardly be said the floodgates had been opened. Entries continued to be modest before the First World War. However, women's tennis in the long skirts era must not be dismissed as mere patball. Lottie Dod, five times champion, was said to have a forehand drive as powerful as any man's. Mrs Dorothea Lambert Chambers, seven times champion and the last before the First World War, came back in 1919 at the age of 41 to face the challenge of Suzanne Lenglen and went down only 8-10, 6-4, 7-9. Lenglen is still declared by all who saw her as the greatest – Wimbledon singles champion six times, doubles six times and mixed doubles three times; French champion twice, world hard courts champion four times and winner of two Olympic gold medals. After Lenglen became a professional in 1926 the American, Helen Wills Moody, was supreme for a decade: eight times singles champion at Wimbledon, seven times in the US and four times in France.

In 1945 women's tennis really took off. There is no space to catalogue all the stars here, but above all must surely come Maureen Connolly. A computer recently matched her and Lenglen as the two all-time greatest, but baulked at the task of deciding which was the greater.

The roll goes on with Margaret Smith (Mrs Court), of Australia, winner of 33 singles titles around the world; Billie Jean King, 19 times a winner at Wimbledon, including six singles titles;

continued on page 60

Champions start young! Sue Barker (far right), from Paignton, Devon, was in the world top ten at the age of 20 by winning French and German singles titles. Virginia Ruzici (centre), Romania's No 1, was already an international veteran at 18. Kerry Reid (above right), of Australia, has won Wimbledon, Australian, West German and South African doubles titles. Tracy Austin (below right) has won many big events around the world, but, so far, only one Wimbledon title: mixed doubles, partnered by her brother, John.

The ladies of the court

continued from page 58

Chris Evert (Mrs Lloyd), for long a world No 1 and
Wimbledon champion; her conqueror there, Martina
Navratilova, champion in 1978 and 1979; and the
charming Evonne Goolagong (Mrs Cawley), who
came to Wimbledon in 1970 and made no impression,
returned in 1971 to win, aged 19 and in 1980
won yet again, the first mother to do so since
1914. Britain's stars have been Wimbledon winners
Angela Mortimer, Anne Jones and Virginia Wade.

Now a new generation of potential champions is
coming along. The established stars look over
their shoulders and see the rapidly rising
youngsters, such as Tracy Austin, already winner
of big money prizes, and Pam Schriver.

With rich rewards to be won, competition gets
keener and standards higher all the time.

Champions on parade: Billie Jean King and Rosemary
Casals (main picture), for long recognised as one of
the most formidable doubles teams, won at Wimbledon
five times and are the only pair to win US titles on
grass, clay, hard court and wood. Martina Navratilova
(above right), Czech refugee now living in the US,
won Wimbledon in 1978 and 1979 from her rival Chris Lloyd
(centre). Britain's Virginia Wade (far right) loyally
saluted Jubilee Year 1977 by winning Wimbledon. Evonne
Cawley (below right) was queen of Wimbledon in 1971
and again in 1980. Below, a potential threat to them
all: exceptionally tall, up-and-coming Pam Schriver

The volley

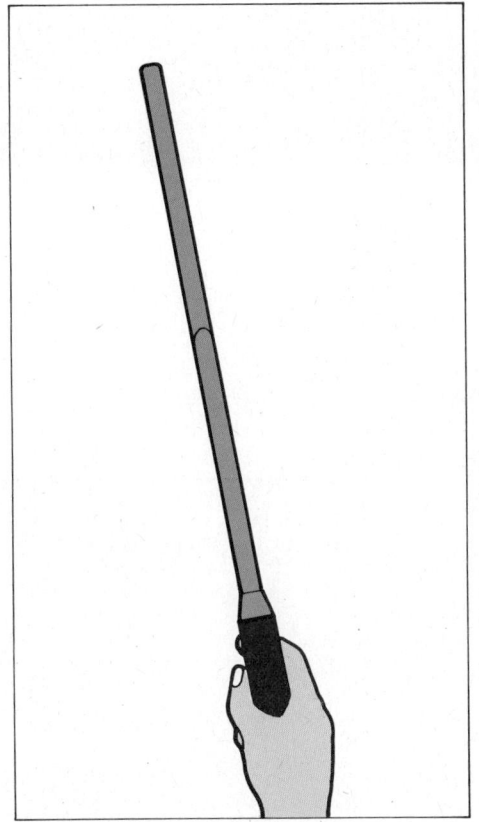

▲ When you first start to play, control volley forehands with the normal eastern forehand grip

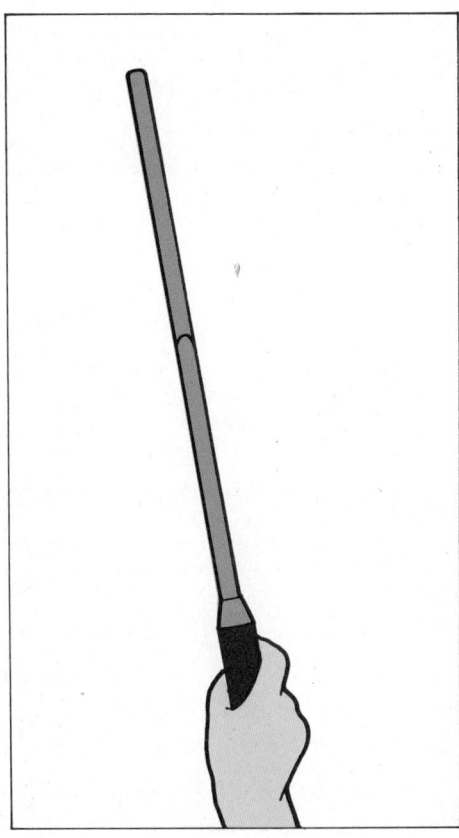

▲ In a more advanced game, you won't have time to change grips; use the 'chopper' service grip for volleys

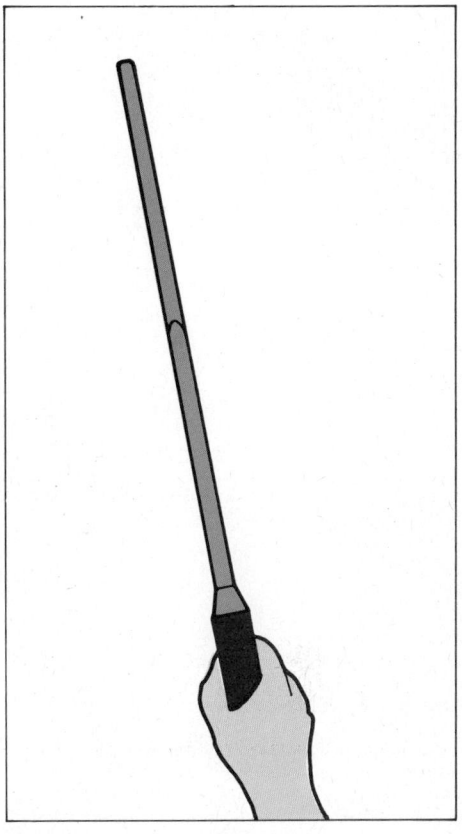

▲ While you are still a beginner, change to the normal backhand grip for a backhand volley

To practise volleys, persuade someone to feed you both forehand and backhand balls as you stand at the net. From the base line, the feeder may find it easier to throw underarm than hurl overarm, as shown in these two diagrams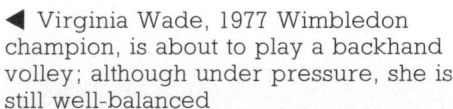

◀ Virginia Wade, 1977 Wimbledon champion, is about to play a backhand volley; although under pressure, she is still well-balanced

The volley is normally an attacking shot from the net, from where you hope to volley the ball out of your opponent's reach.

When first starting to volley you may change grips as you would on ground strokes, to obtain better control of the racket head but, once your tennis reaches a reasonable level, the game will be too fast for you to change grips and you will use only the 'chopper' service grip.

Basic position for the volleyer is a racket length and a pace (about 1·20-1·50m or 4-5ft)

from the net. (When playing tennis you should preferably be either at the back of the court or in at the net, not at mid-court where your opponent will find it easy to pass you or to hit the ball at your feet.)

There are two types of volley: where the ball comes above the height of the net and can be punched down in an attacking shot; and when it dips below the level of the net and has just to be kept in play with a firm push, hit with an open racket face.

The forehand volley

Correct grip for a volley – between backhand and forehand grips, once the speed of the game is too fast to change grips

The forehand grip at this level is incorrect – no good for a backhand and no time to change it

▲ The volleyer is standing square to the net in the basic ready position, very much on her toes, ready to pounce on a ball coming to either side of her or from above. The ideal volleying position is about a racket length and a pace back from the net so that you are close enough to punch the ball downwards without hitting the net with your racket, which would lose you the point

▲ The ball is on her forehand and she has stepped on to her right foot while taking the racket a short way back with the racket head up and a firm, cocked wrist. She is going to punch the ball down over the net

The attacking forehand volley (shown above) From the ready position at the net, when your opponent's ball reaches you above the height of the net, take a short back swing (you have neither time nor necessity for more); keeping a firm grip and cocked wrist so that the racket head is up, step in and take the ball early. The

ball should be taken slightly in front of you and punched down with a flat racket face and a short follow-through.

The shot should be played with a firm wrist, the racket head above it

Do not drop the racket head below your wrist; make sure you bend your knees instead

▲ She is taking the volley slightly in front of her and hitting the ball with the racket face flat. She has stepped in to take the shot early and is putting her weight into it, with both knees slightly bent

▲ She has made a short follow-through, keeping a firm wrist and taking the weight on her left foot. A long follow-through might well have taken the ball out of court; a relaxed wrist would probably have put the ball into the net. She must now get into the basic ready position again, if she can, before her shot is returned

The low forehand volley (pictured in the series below) is treated differently. You are probably on your way to the net from a service or a ground stroke and your opponent has hit a topspin return to your feet which you can just reach before it bounces. Bend your knees so that you can keep the racket head up, take a short back swing, open the racket face so that the ball will travel upwards over the net and play it slightly in front of you. Finish with a short follow-through, then continue smoothly to the net to take up a better position in which to volley.

The backhand volley

Stand about a racket length and a pace back from the net to volley

If you stand too near the net you may touch it with your racket and so lose the point

▲ The volleyer stands in the ready position, facing the net and about 1·20-1·50m (4-5ft) from it, racket head up and both hands on the shaft. (If you are moving in to the net, steady yourself to play the volley and then move on; if you hit the ball while running, you could lose control of the shot)

▲ The ball is coming on his backhand. He has turned sideways to the ball and taken the racket back with both hands in a short back swing, because he does not have time for a full swing – nor is it necessary, as a short punch at the ball is effective. A beginner can change to a backhand grip, but later should adopt the 'chopper' service grip for all volleys on either side

Most players find the backhand volley more difficult than the forehand at first. Your wrist is probably not strong enough yet and you will have to play a lot of volleys before it feels comfortable. At first, you can use the backhand grip to give you better control but, as you progress, you should use the 'chopper' service grip at the net all the time.

You should position your feet, balance yourself and use your weight as for a ground stroke backhand (see page 32)

The attacking backhand volley (shown above) is possible when the ball reaches you above net height. With a short back swing, punch at the ball, taking it early in front of your body and

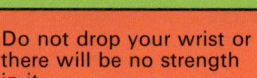

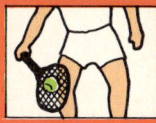

▲ He is well balanced, playing the volley off his leading foot and taking the ball early, just in front of the right leg. He has released his left hand from the shaft to swing at the ball. His wrist is cocked, with the racket head up and flat to the ball

▲ He has punched at the ball with a short follow-through. His left hand is coming forward to clasp the racket shaft again and lend support to its positioning for the next shot

hitting with a slightly open racket face. Keep the racket head above your firm, cocked wrist and finish with a short follow-through.

The low backhand volley (pictured in the series below) The same principles apply, but you must bend your knees low to take the ball as you open (tilt) the racket face, so that the ball clears the net.

In the first photograph, in the series below, the player is too upright as she volleys; in the second, the author shows her how to open her racket face. In the third, he shows her how to bend low to keep the racket head up and her wrist cocked. In the last photograph she is bearing these points in mind and getting a better, but not yet perfect, result.

The half-volley

The racket head should be kept firm and parallel to the ground

The wrist must be cocked and firm as you lift the ball over the net

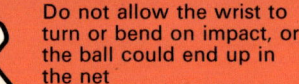

Do not allow the wrist to turn or bend on impact, or the ball could end up in the net

The racket head must not be dropped or you will probably lose control

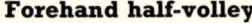

Forehand half-volley

▲ The player has bent very low, sideways to the ball, with his head right over it, racket parallel to the ground. (If you bend low enough, you may scrape your knuckles – showing that you have the right approach!)

▲ He is keeping his wrist firm and cocked and his head down as he lifts the ball on the strings in order to get it over the net and deep to the back of the court

▲ He is following-through high with his racket and staying with the ball as long as possible. His weight has come forward on to his leading foot; he will continue to a safer position at the net

The author has served and moved towards the net, but a good return has caught him mid-court (left). He bends low, sideways to the ball, keeping his head over it. He lifts the ball up (above) and as far as he can to the back of the court and continues his approach to the net

68

Do not let the racket head drop on impact or on the follow-through

Backhand half-volley

▲ The ball has landed low at the player's feet. He has turned sideways to it and is bending low so that he can keep his wrist firm with the racket parallel to the ground. He takes hardly any back swing

▲ He follows the ball through as far as possible so that he really feels the ball on the strings and has more control over it. His weight is on his forward foot, elbow straight

▲ He is finishing the shot with a high follow-through to get as much depth on the shot as possible and he is already preparing to finish his run up to a better position at the net

The half-volley, when the ball is hit just after it bounces, is one of the most difficult shots in the game, because you are right on top of the bouncing ball, without the opportunity to move forward for a volley or back for a ground stroke. You need lightning judgment. You usually have to play it as you are running in to the net.

To play a half-volley, steady yourself and bend your knees as low as possible. With almost no back swing, and keeping the racket parallel to the ground, lift the ball over the net. Keep your head over it for as long as possible and continue carrying the ball on the strings with an extended follow-through. Your wrist must remain firm.

Do not look for winners off this difficult shot, but try to play the ball deep to the back of the court to give you time to get into a better position.

If you find yourself having to play a lot of half-volleys, you are probably misjudging your approaches to the net and should review tactics.

Demonstrating three stages of a backhand half-volley: the short swing back, bent knees, racket parallel to the ground, and the start of the long follow-through necessary to lift the ball up over the net and deep to the back of the court. Strong legs are needed!

The lob

The defensive lob

▲ The ball is landing over the player's head so she is moving back quickly, watching the ball all the way. While she is running she will judge where it will bounce and start taking her racket back ready for the shot

▲ She has run back into position, swinging the racket back so that she can get the face under the ball. To get the necessary height, the racket face is open so that she can lift the ball high into the air

▲ She is using a long, high follow-through to get the ball high and deep enough to clear her opponent, keeping the ball on the strings as long as possible. It is better to get too much height than too little, to give yourself time to recover

If your opponent has hit a good return and is at the net waiting to pounce on your reply, you should lob the ball, lifting it high in the air and over his head to give yourself time to recover your position.

To hit a lob, place yourself sideways to the ball, weight on your back foot, open the racket face and lift the ball high and, if possible, over your opponent's reach. If he manages to smash your lob then – from behind your base line – block the ball back, keeping the wrist firm and the racket face open and trying to give the ball height. After two or three of these lobbed returns it is amazing how difficult your opponent will find it to smash!

Use topspin on a lob as an attacking shot to whisk the ball over your opponent's head and run it away from him on its bounce. When your opponent goes back to retrieve your lob, move straight in to the net to attack his return.

If you hold the racket face open (tilted), it will be a normal lob with backspin, (opposite) not topspin

The racket face should be flat as it brushes up the back of the ball to make it spin forward

If you don't use a lot of force, you won't get enough height on the ball

The topspin lob

▲ The player has positioned himself sideways to the shot and is taking his racket low so that he can brush up the back of the ball with a flat racket face.

▲ To obtain height and spin on the ball, he is taking the racket face almost straight up, weight pressing on his forward foot and bent leg. The ball will lift over his opponent and then dip and bound away on bouncing

▲ Because he is trying to make the ball 'fizz' with extreme spin, his racket face has finished over his right shoulder; normally you can get a good spin and finish the follow-through over on your left

Left, the author bends low to lob with open racket face; above, his opponent shows the high follow-through as she lobs over his head from the back of the court; and, in the picture opposite, the player is executing a normal lob in much the same position as that in the third diagram

The smash

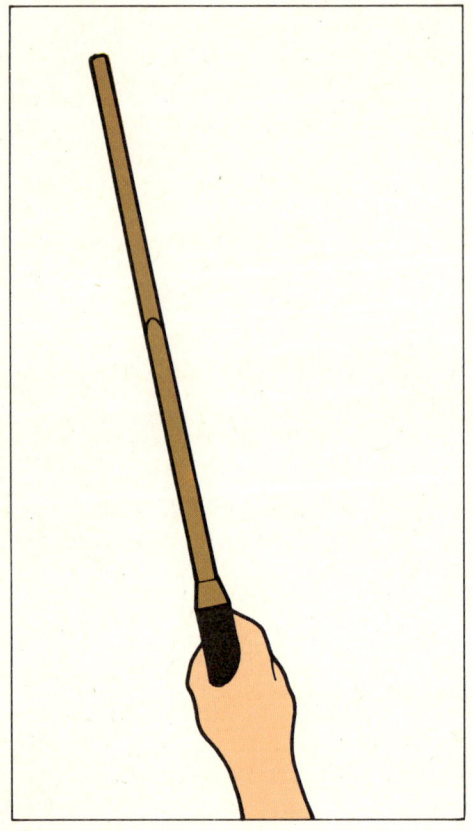

▲ He uses the normal 'chopper' service grip, held loosely so that his wrist can give that extra pace needed for a really fierce smash. It allows him to hit the ball with the racket face turned slightly inwards, which gives more control to the shot

▲ He stands correctly in the volley position at the net. (Never lurk somewhere near the service line, anticipating a lob; your opponent may hit the shot at your feet instead and then he will be the one attacking you!)

▲ His opponent has lobbed the ball, so he moves back sideways, racket head up, watching the ball all the time. Sideways moving allows him to take longer strides and to be in the basic sideways serving position when he hits the ball

The smash, a forceful overhead shot, can be one of the most satisfying shots to play.

From your volleying position at the net, from the way your opponent prepares to play his shot, you read that a lob is coming. He will be trying to lift the ball over you, and, as the ball leaves his racket, you should already be moving back quickly and sideways to be underneath the ball as it drops, ready for a forehand smash. With your normal service 'chopper' grip, take the racket *up* and over your right shoulder, dropping the head behind your back. Point your left arm at the ball, both to judge it and balance yourself, watching it closely all the way. Throw the racket head at the ball, with its face turned slightly in (i.e. towards the left-hand net post) to

Practise smashing by having your partner feed you balls from his racket or by having him throw the ball into the air, underarm or overarm, from the base line (or service line if he is very brave). Start at the net with easy smashes, then gradually progress to the ball being thrown higher and deeper into court to make the smashes more difficult. To prevent monotony, a good practice is to play competitively, scoring a point a rally, with the one who is practising smashing not allowed to let the ball bounce ▶

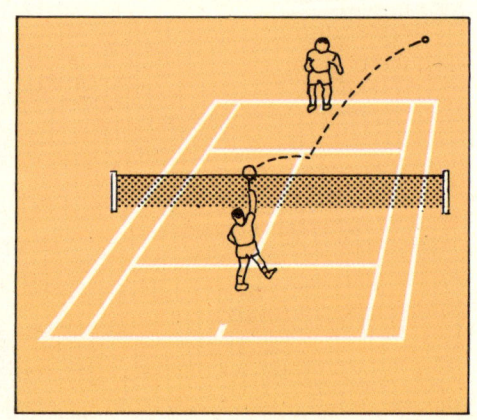

▲ He is taking the racket up and back over his right shoulder (not down and back, as he would to serve) and pointing at the ball with his left hand, which will help him to judge it on to the racket head

▲ He is now in the correct position to hit the ball just in front of him so that he can hit it downwards into court. Positioning is vital – if he takes the ball too far back he will hit upwards and out; too far forward and he will hit it into the net

▲ He has finished his smash nicely balanced, having hit the ball at the top of his reach and taken the racket face across his body, so that he has followed the ball right through. His weight is now transferred to his forward foot

help control the ball, hitting it at arm's length and just in front of you, taking the racket through and down. Put your weight into the shot and on to your leading foot as you hit. Make certain you finish in balance, without falling about. A skilled player can smash with a flat racket face, giving much less control, and will also sometimes put a reverse spin on the ball by angling his racket outwards.

The same principles apply to the more difficult backhand smash, but this time concentrate on keeping grip and wrist firm.

The skill of your opponent's lob will determine whether you can smash away a winner, or just play the ball firmly back to enable you to regain the net. The vital factor in both smashes is to move to the right position under the ball.

For the difficult high backhand smash, you need to hold the racket more firmly and to keep a firm wrist ▶

The drop shot

The racket head should be laid back to hit underneath the ball and impart as much backspin as possible

If the racket face is too flat there will be little spin on the ball and it will bounce straight on for an easy return

▲ The player is about to take his racket back in the conventional forehand loop, as if to make a normal forehand drive. He hopes his opponent will be deceived into thinking he is preparing to hit a drive deep to the back of the court

▲ As he comes through with the racket, he lays his wrist back and opens the racket face, so that he hits the underneath part of the ball to make it spin backwards; on landing, it will bounce vertically or, ideally, it will bounce backwards

▲ His follow-through is short, but his racket has stayed with the ball as long as possible and he is keeping his wrist firm. His weight has transferred to his leading foot in the usual way so that he is balanced throughout the shot

The drop shot is hit with backspin, to drop short over the net and die with very little bounce; it is played when your opponent is at the back of the court and has hit a fairly weak drive, giving you the opportunity to play this delicate touch shot.

Prepare as you would for a normal forehand or backhand drive, to disguise your intentions, but come through much more slowly, with open racket face and laid back wrist, to hit the bottom of the ball and give it a great deal of backspin. Bend your head to watch the ball on to the strings and caress it just over the net. Keep your wrist firm and finish with a short follow-through.

This shot needs a lot of practising, for your margin of error is small; if hit too high or too hard it makes an easy return for your opponent, if not hard enough it will not go over the net. If played well, it can win a rally outright.

She is playing a backhand drop shot, slicing under the ball with a short follow-through ▶

▲ Here we see leading lady player Chris Lloyd playing one of her devastating drop shots. Nicely balanced, sideways to the direction of her shot, she has her wrist laid well back, with the racket face open so that she can brush it under the ball, spinning the ball backwards so much that it will almost stop when hitting the court, and land short, to the confusion of her opponent

The player at this end of the court has hit a deep drive to ▶ move his opponent to one side of the court; the opponent's return is comparatively weak and short, enabling the player to play a drop shot to the opposite side; his opponent will have to move very fast to reach the ball and play a reasonable shot

Extra and extraordinary shots

The shots which have been discussed so far are the basic requirements of any player who wishes to attain the great enjoyment from the game that having a variety of shots allows him. There are many other shots used by talented, if unorthodox, players.

The most important feature of tennis is to hit the ball back into court. Those of us who have played tennis for a long time will have come across the player who displays some beautifully fluent strokes as you knock up before the match, yet hardly wins a game because he is not prepared to improvise. My regular doubles partner, David Olney, is always growling at me to hack the ball back into court no matter how, and this is what the game is all about. Ideally, play the ball with as correct a technique as possible, but also accept that there will be times when you must get the ball back with the wrong grip, off the wrong foot, or with the racket head dropped.

The two world-class players in our pictures, Francoise Durr (overleaf) and Frew McMillan (opposite) are both extremely unorthodox, but they have obtained splendid results at world level. Francoise Durr, who has won the French title, plays with her index finger along the back of the racket for her ground strokes and volleys, and hits her service with a frying-pan grip! McMillan has double-handed backhands, forehands and volleys and for several years – during which he won the Wimbledon men's doubles three times with Bob Hewitt – was acknowledged to be the world's leading left court player.

If Durr and McMillan had had orthodox coaching, might they have been better players? Or is it just *because* they are unorthodox that they have been so successful?

Mike Francis, a leading British county player, plays all his shots with the same side of the racket face, hitting forehands with a western grip and just rolling his wrist over backwards for his backhands!

Venture to play an unorthodox shot as necessary. Often the talk in the dressing-room after the match is about the incredible topspin passing shot hit on the run; the dink played one way while looking the other; the volley returned with the racket behind you, or the rally won with eight consecutive lobs.

Always bear in mind, though, that it is the player playing sensible 'bread and butter' tennis who generally wins.

▲ The author prepares to play a stop volley with backspin

Frew McMillan, who plays double-handed on both sides ▶

▼ Playing off the wrong foot and leaning backwards too!

Extra and extraordinary shots

▲ When the ball is hit straight at you, protect yourself and return the ball with a backhand volley. If you try a forehand, you could well miss the ball *and* get hit!

▲ A reverse spin smash. Change the normal 'chopper' grip to a western forehand (see page 20) and smash the ball with the racket face angled outwards, rather than flat or inwards

▲ Improvisation. She has had to stretch for the ball and has dropped her racket head to do so – but the ball is returned safely into court

▲ A wide backhand return from Francoise Durr, the French No 1. Notice the unconventional grip, with the index finger along the back of the racket, and the bent wrist

▲ With the ball coming low at his feet, his quick reaction is to flip the ball back with the racket behind him

▲ Deception, with the player looking one way (to wrong-foot his opponent) and the ball going the other

▲ In a fast exchange at the net, the player reacts by volleying the ball from behind on the backhand side

The men who make the headlines

It's tough at the top. The men who make the tennis headlines need stamina. About 100 chase a share of the annual multi-million-dollar prize packet. They have to fight hard to reach the top – and harder to stay there

Who is the greatest player of all time? The experts cannot agree, but most of them settle for two: 'Big Bill' Tilden and Rod 'the Rocket' Laver. They had one thing in common: a decade at the top before they slipped back. Today the average is about six years.

The classic performers still rise, though life at the top is more precarious than it was when Laver emerged with his first Australian title in 1960.

Jimmy Connors has had his share of ups and downs. He won the US indoors and South African championships in 1973 at the age of 20. In 1974 he had a tremendous run: champion of Australia, South Africa, Wimbledon and US Open, on clay courts and indoors. In 1975 he lost them all except the indoors and dropped in world ranking to No 2. In 1977 he was back at the top, world and US No 1. But the younger Borg – 'Jimbo' is four years older – has caught up. Connors has always been a fighter and he isn't finished yet, but . . . time marches on.

It caught up with Arthur Ashe, who crowned a career that included the US Championship (1968), and Australian (1970) by winning Wimbledon in 1975, using his artistry to overcome Connors' power when he was already past 30. However, after a great opening run in 1976, he slipped, lost Wimbledon and dropped out of the top ten.

Singles champions tend to occupy the limelight, but occasionally there comes a historic doubles team, like Hewitt and McMillan. Bob Hewitt, an Australian, emigrated to South Africa

continued on page 83

Action by Jimmy Connors demonstrates the power play of the top class men's game. Nevertheless, the artistry of Arthur Ashe (far right, top) overcame the younger, stronger Connors at Wimbledon in 1975. John McEnroe (far right, bottom), is one of the powerful contenders for top honours. John Lloyd (right) was No 2 in Britain's Davis Cup team, overwhelmed by McEnroe's Americans

The men who make the headlines

continued from page 80

and teamed up with Fred McMillan in 1967 – their greatest year when they became champions of South Africa, British Hard Courts, Italy, Wimbledon and Germany. That was their first Wimbledon triumph, to be repeated in 1972 and 1978, an astonishing run at the top, which included the 1977 US Open title.

John McEnroe presents a challenge in both singles and doubles. His era has been dominated by Connors and Borg and although he has defeated both in top class events, including the World Championship Tennis finals, he has yet to win the Wimbledon crown. His losing final to Borg in 1980 was an epic performance that held 14,000 Centre Court spectators enthralled to the last shot.

Sadly, British men's tennis has been a disappointment since Fred Perry's heyday. In 1978 Britain reached the Davis Cup final thanks to our Nos 1 and 2, 'Buster' Mottram and John Lloyd, but the team was hopelessly outclassed by the US led by the powerful McEnroe. Wimbledon's not inconsiderable profits all flow back into the 'grass roots' to train and develop young players. We can only hope this will alter Britain's sorry plight – soon. Another Perry is badly needed.

The great Hewitt-McMillan doubles team in action (main picture). 'Buster' Mottram (inset, far left), is Britain's unchallenged No 1 and (centre) the temperamental Ilie Nastase is always a crowd-puller. Vitas Gerulaitis (left) won Wimbledon doubles (with A. Mayer) in 1975 and ousted champion Ashe in 1976. John Newcombe (below), one of Wimbledon's greatest, was champion in 1967, 1970 and 1971

Tactics of the game

Many of us think that tennis is the finest game of all. It can be a team game, with either sex as your partner, or an individual contest. There are many different levels at which you can play, for it is not an easy game to master, and this makes it all the more enjoyable as you attain a reasonable standard.

Over a hundred years ago when the game started, it was played at garden parties for fun and exercise. Soon more competitive players realized that here was a sport they could get their teeth into; the less competitive had a sport which could be great fun on a lovely summer's day. No wonder it has such a wide following among all age-groups.

There are four possible venues for play: the public courts; sports centres, now springing up all over the country; the local tennis club (usually offering amazing value for money); or your own court, if you are lucky.

You can learn the game at moderate expense. There are many highly competent coaches in the game, and at most large clubs qualified coaches teach groups of people at very reasonable prices. There are also sponsored national coaching schemes for promising players. With the coverage of big events on TV and radio, you can learn the finer points of the game.

At first a learner will find it exhilarating just to get the ball over the net and to the spot he intended. As he improves, he will appreciate tactics and angles; he will learn to play his opponent like a fish, from side to side, and backwards and forwards (remembering his opponent is trying to do the same); he will try to wrong-foot his opponent by disguising the direction of his shots. As he plays, he will work several moves ahead in his mind. In doubles, he will mind-read his partner's moves so that he can quickly position himself in relation to him. At the net he will 'move with the bounce' of the ball to cover the area of court to which his opponent can angle the return. It is easy to become absorbed in the game and this concentration in itself is a great asset.

In the ensuing pages you will find some suggestions which will open your mind to tactical possibilities.

Today top tennis is truly international and its epic contests are fought out on courts across the world. Here Alex Metreveli of the USSR confronts Jimmy Connors of the USA, on a court in England ►

Singles

Before playing a singles, calculate your own (and your opponent's) fitness, capabilities in technique and the type of court on which you are to play. It is no good planning to knock your opponent off court with a serve-volley game if your volleys are weak and his returns good, or trying to out-steady him if his ground strokes are more reliable than yours.

Try to practise all your strokes before a match. The top players do this and warm themselves up with exercises. Treat the knock-up as a tactical part of it; practise all the shots in your repertoire, and at the same time check your opponent's game for possible weaknesses.

Generally, on a grass or indoor court you should volley a lot and consistently play attacking ground strokes, as the ball will move fast off these surfaces. When playing on a slow hard court, where the ball grips the court and bounces higher, you must expect longer rallies and be more selective in hitting attacking ground strokes and in approaching the net.

During the match, sound out all your opponent's basic strokes. Consider whether you should vary the pace of your own. Do not tire yourself by rushing about between points. On big points – game points, set points and match points – really concentrate.

There will be many occasions when you should obtain great satisfaction even though you lose the match, for if you have tried every shot and tactic you know and chased every ball and still lost, then you have been beaten by the better player on the day.

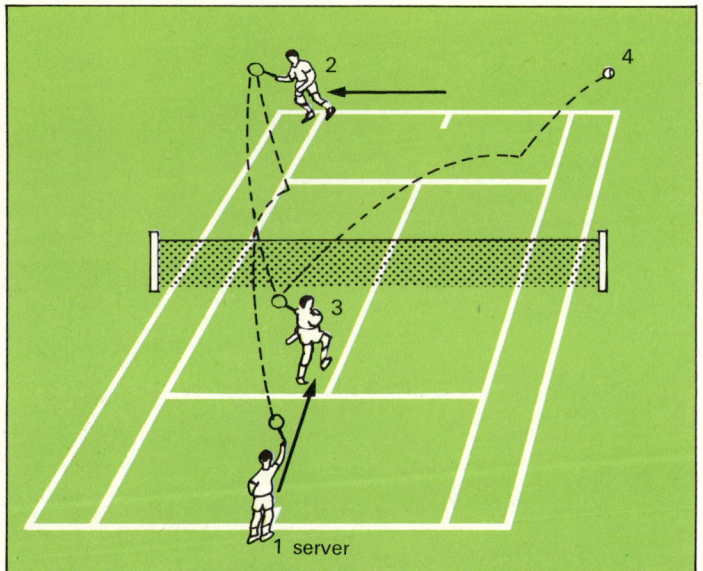

In these diagrams, the shots are numbered in sequence from the serve; the flight of the ball is shown by dotted lines; and the players' moves are arrowed.

Above The ideal service tactic, where you ace your opponent by hitting your fast first service into the corner of the service box so that he cannot reach it. (You can practise this by placing targets in the corners of the service boxes and serving at them)

Above right Another serving tactic. You serve the ball wide, taking your opponent out of court, and follow your service to the net. You volley his return into the empty, opposite corner

Right This time you decide to follow your service up to the net, albeit rather slowly. The receiver returns down the side line and you wrong-foot your opponent, who is returning to a central position, by playing the ball back to the same place

◄ Always decide before you serve whether you are going to stay back or move in to the net. If you follow your service in, move as fast as possible (photograph far left) without foot-faulting, so that you can volley the return from inside the service box (middle photograph; from this low angle the volley should be deep to the back of the court), then move in to the net position to give your opponent less of an angle to pass you, and so that you can punch away the fifth shot of the rally from above the height of the net (near photograph). When receiving service, you should aim to control into court the faster first service and attack the probably weaker second service

Again, the strokes are numbered in sequence in these diagrams; the dotted lines show the flight of the ball, and arrows show players' directional moves

Above left A receiver's tactic. The server has opted to stay back after serving. You return the ball wide across court to take the server out of court, and you follow your return to the net. On the fourth stroke of the rally you volley the ball to his opposite corner for a winner

Above This time the server follows the ball to the net and, after returning it, so do you. Having 'read' where he is going to place his volley, you are able to reach it and punch it into the open space at the back of the court

Left The server has hit a weak second service, and you take advantage of it with an attacking forehand to his backhand, then run in to the net. You volley his backhand return to the opposite corner

Doubles

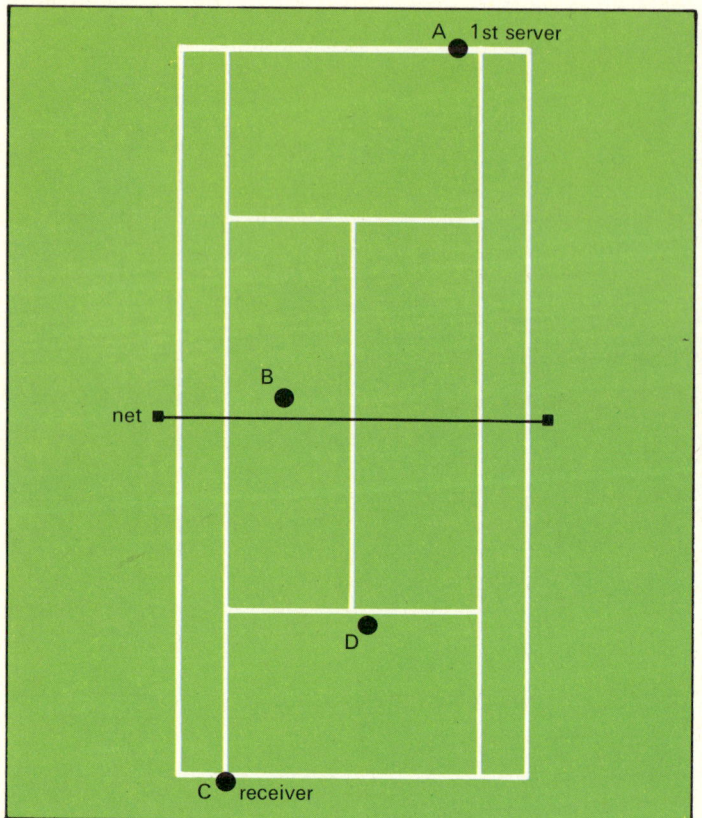

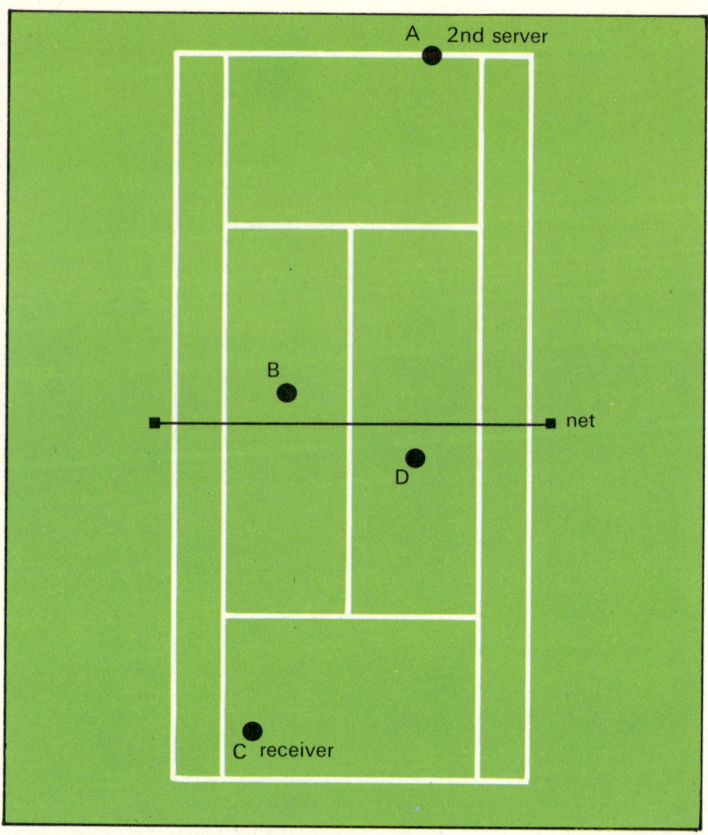

▲ A serves from near the tramlines to obtain a better angle on C's backhand, and for A to hit a forehand should C return the ball to him. A's partner B is at the net

▲ A's first service was a fault so C moves forward to attack A's second service. The receiver's partner D also moves forward, hoping to attack the third shot

When serving in doubles, the server stands a little further from the base line centre mark than he does for singles. His partner usually stands at the net, covering his half of the court and also ready to pounce across to his partner's side to intercept a weak return. The service can, with advantage, be directed down the centre to limit the angle of return, or to the receiver's usually weaker backhand (or both). The server aims to join his partner in the attack at the net.

The opposing pair also aim to dominate at the net. The person receiving service stands behind or just inside the base line, depending on the speed of service, while his partner stands at mid-court, ready to move as the situation demands, preferably up to the net. They try to advance and retreat in parallel.

Each player moves to cover the area of court left open when his partner runs for a shot, and equally moves to cover an opponent's return of a wide ball on the side he is covering.

The best pairs talk and motivate each other during the game. They know each other's play so well there are no misunderstandings about who will hit the ball, especially the one that comes down the centre between them.

▲ The server serves down the middle, to minimize the angle of return. The server runs in and volleys the third stroke of the rally across court, avoiding the forward player; the basic doubles shot is always across court

◀ Potential winners. Top, the server's partner leaps across from his attacking position at the net to intercept the return of service. Below, the author is intercepting the incoming server's first volley, off the author's partner's attacking return of service

▲ The server stays back. The returner lobs the server's partner at the net. The server moves across to play the lob, and his partner moves back to cover the opposite side. When the server plays the third shot of the rally, the returning pair should both have run in to the net

Men's doubles

▲ The server moves in fast to the net. His partner is lobbed, but chases the lob rather than move across, as he would do had his partner not followed his serve. The server has time to move back to be in line with his partner, and the returning pair take advantage of this to move up to dominate the net

Beginners in doubles usually serve and stand just behind the base line but as soon as their game improves, in men's doubles especially, they follow service to the net and try to volley or smash every shot. The server's partner will try to help win the game by intercepting, or moving as if to intercept, at the net, and the receiver's partner will be doing the same.

Normally the server has the advantage, so wins the game – 'holds service'; if he should lose, this is a 'service break' and is often decisive in the result of the match.

The server should concentrate on getting a high percentage of first services and first volleys into court. The returner should aim to hit every return back into court, low at the server's feet if he is coming in to the net.

If in trouble, start throwing high lobs, with both you and your partner well behind the base line and, should your opponents let the ball bounce before hitting it, you should both speed to the net to regain the attack.

◄ If the volleying pair hit the ball well to the left or the right, and then both move in that direction, it needs a superb cross-court return to pass them

▼ The server has followed his service in to join his partner and, nicely balanced, is preparing to play a firm first volley back to the receiver

▲ This is called the Australian formation (and is quite legal); the server's partner stands on the same side of the court as the server and the server, after serving, moves *across* court to the net. This tactic is generally used when the receiver's return of service across court is too good for the incoming server to volley at all comfortably on his way up to the net

91

Ladies' doubles

▲ A top ladies' doubles, with the left-handed server standing near the tramlines so that she can slice the ball to her opponent's backhand

▲ Not the ideal positioning (dots indicate the players), but one which happens more frequently in ladies' doubles, where ground strokes are usually more reliable

Only at the very top level do women players follow their services to the net every time, possibly because they are not quite as strong or mobile as men. So ladies' doubles are all about consistent ground strokes, good lobs and steady serving. Rallies last longer, and the usual formation is for each pair to have one player at the back of the court and one at the net, with long cross-court rallies, the two net players bobbing in and out, looking to cut off the ground stroke rallies with volleys.

The better player usually should play in the left court to receive service, as the most vital returns will be from here – at 40-love, 40-30, or advantage; she can also take on her forehand balls that come down the centre, between her and her partner. An exception is the player who has an unusually fierce forehand, when it may be advantageous to receive on the right.

If a particularly fierce drive has been hit, the player under pressure at the back of the court may lob the player at the net. The net player then crosses to cover the other half of the court and her partner at the back crosses to take the lob.

If one of the opposing players is much weaker, as much as possible of the play should be directed at her. This applies to all doubles match play.

The ideal ladies' doubles player has sound ground strokes, a consistent serve, a good lob, the ability to intercept, a shrewd tactical brain – and a great deal of patience!

Top: The correct positions for the serving pair.
Above: The pair at the net are covering the centre and left of their court, as the ball will be coming from that side.
Right: The normal ladies' doubles formation, with two players exchanging cross-court drives

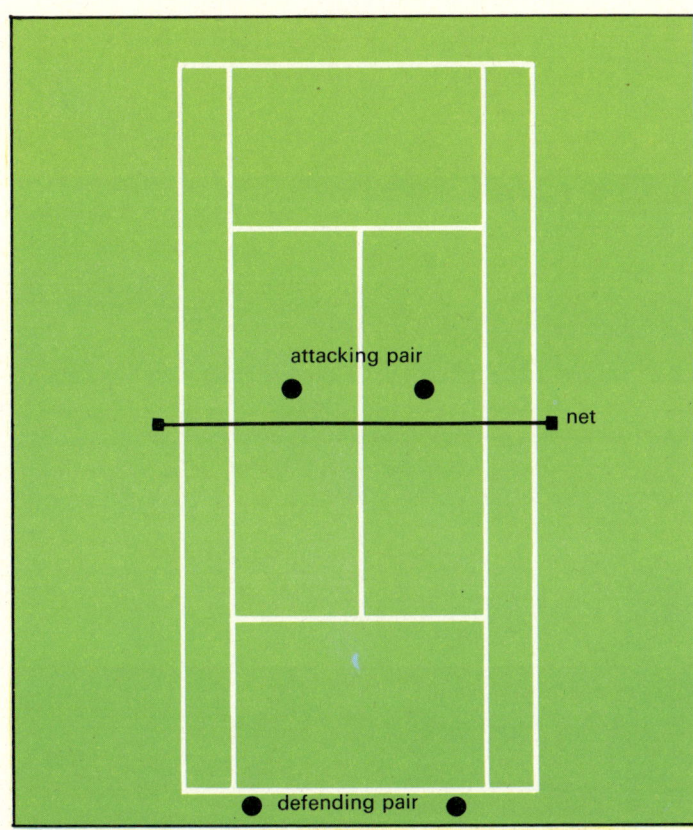

attacking pair

net

defending pair

▲ Better tactically, with the attacking pair at the net, volleying and smashing, and the defending pair behind the base line, chasing and lobbing for all they are worth

net

▲ The ultimate in doubles, with all four players having reached the net for a volleying rat-a-tat-tat. They stand a little back from the net for room to react

Mixed doubles

▼ The player serves from the far left of the court, to be able to play a forehand should her opponent return the ball across court to her. Her partner is ready to pounce on any loose return, moving with the bounce of the serve to cover the angle of return

▲ The player following his service to the net is thwarted by a lob over his partner's head. He stops and chases back across court to the lob, his partner crosses over and back to cover, and the returning pair will probably move in to the net to attack

The server hits the ball down the centre to the receiver's ▲ backhand, and the server's partner is able to move over to intercept. In the sequence on the right, the pair at the far end are lobbed down the line, and the man moves back while his partner crosses over

Tactically, mixed doubles is the most difficult of the doubles games to play. Normally in each pair the man will be the stronger player, and he will usually chase all the lobs and take the smashes. Both partnerships will try to play on the weaker opponent, and both stronger players will try to take a major part of the shots. This makes the tactics more complex, and the players must consider carefully the right time to intercept, to lob, to play a cross-court return or to hit down the line.

The stronger player should take the left court when receiving service so that he can cover more of the court from the left side and play the important service points. He should have a tacit agreement with his partner that he takes most of the central shots.

To make it easier for your partner to intercept, serve down the centre of the court or to your opponent's weaker side. If you find your opponents cutting off your returns at the net, vary your strokes with a mixture of lobs, cross-court drives and shots down the line (but remember the net is higher at the sides).

The elusive Grand Slam

The Grand Slam! That is supreme world champion play, to win the Australian, French, Wimbledon and US titles in the same year. Only two men and two women have succeeded in singles. All four are tennis greats: Donald Budge in 1938; Rod Laver in 1962 and again in 1969; Maureen Connolly, 1953; and Mrs Margaret Court, 1970

Winning the Grand Slam calls for more than just skill and concentration. Many great players have been on the verge, only to see the prize slip away. The Australian Jack Crawford was the first man almost to achieve it, in 1933. After Wimbledon he needed only Forest Hills – but that was to be Fred Perry's year in the US, where he was the first British winner there since 1903. Then in 1934 it was Perry's turn to be thwarted – ousted unexpectedly and early in France.

So to 1938 and the first name enrolled on the scroll of honour: Donald Budge. With Perry out of the way, Budge won all three Wimbledon titles in 1937, came back in 1938 and repeated the performance without losing a set – and went on to the Grand Slam. An immaculate champion.

In post-war years the competition has been fierce, world standards higher and the slam at first even more elusive. Then Rod Laver took command of world tennis. He stormed to success in 1962 and turned professional when the championships were for amateurs only. Then in 1968 the professionals were welcomed back and in 1969 the Rocket repeated his achievement.

Pre-World War Two, of the great women players only Mrs Helen Wills Moody ever came near – in 1928 and 1929. Then, in 1953, 19-year-old Maureen Connolly came from America to slam her way round the world. In 1970 Mrs Margaret Court of Australia joined her in the list.

Mrs Court had been nearly there three times before with three out of four in 1962, 1965 and 1969; and in 1973 she again won three but lost at Wimbledon.

In mixed doubles Mrs Court and Ken Fletcher, also Australian, achieved the Slam in 1963 and in men's doubles Ken McGregor and Frank Sedgman of Australia brought off the Slam in 1951. Doubles events in which one player has achieved a Slam playing with different partners are: Women's: Maria Bueno, Brazil, 1960; Mixed: Margaret Court 1965; and Owen Davidson, Australia, 1967.

Left-hander Rod Laver gets to an 'impossible' return, displaying the form that brought him two incredible Grand Slams and made him for a decade the world's No 1. Majestic Donald Budge (inset), who was first to achieve the Grand Slam, ranks among the all-time stars

Left-handers

left-handed player receiving

right-handed server

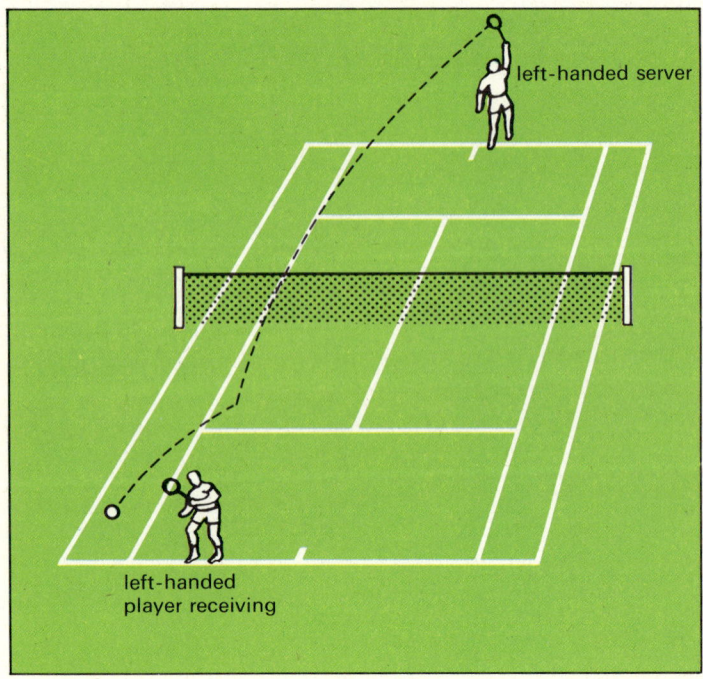

left-handed server

left-handed player receiving

Being a left-hander is worth a 15-points-a-game start! The left-hander's opponent has to adjust his tactical shots to the opposite direction; if he plays his usual game (to a right-hander's backhand) he will find himself playing to the left-hander's strength.

The left-hander himself can afford to put slice on most of his services as this will spin the ball away on an opposing right-hander's backhand. However, he will also need to develop a flat fast service, to ace the right-hander who has started to move too far over to cover the backhand, and for serving to another left-hander's backhand.

The forehand can be developed as a hard cross-court drive with topspin; most left-handers excel on this side. Where they do seem to struggle (although the players pictured here have no problems) is on the backhand, where many appear to have just a chipped return. The 'lefty' should develop a firm sliced backhand, plus one where he hits the ball with topspin. Grand Slam winner and left-hander Rod Laver had one of the greatest backhands of all time, showing what can be achieved.

Volleys are similar to a right-hander's, but opponents should remember to lob to a position that will put the ball on the left-hander's backhand smash, or he will be presented with an easy winner.

Never come off court saying you thought your opponent had a good backhand, to be told that that was not his backhand but his (left-handed) forehand!

▲ Left, the right-hander serves with slice, wide to the left-hander's backhand. Above, the left-hander's sliced service goes deep to the left-hander's forehand

▼ Tony Roche, five times Wimbledon doubles champion

▲ Ann Jones won the Wimbledon championship in 1969

Martina Navratilova, Wimbledon champion in 1978   ▶

▼ Brilliant young star John McEnroe

Fitness

▲ Squat thrusts: hands on floor, jump your feet backwards and forwards, knees straight then bent

▼ Potato race: each player has a row of spaced-out tennis balls. She must pick each up in turn, race back and place it on a racket on the base line

There is no better feeling than to go on court knowing that you are at the peak of your game, 'match tight', in practice and fully fit. If you are to reach a good standard in any sport these days you should get yourself as fit as possible in accordance with your age. In the past we played a sport to get fit; now we get fit to play the sport.

Don't overdo your training at first. Al Murray has a programme at his gymnasium for which he has charted the limits to which your pulse should go. At rest, normal rate is about 72-80 a minute; this shows how hard your heart is working. He reckons 200 a minute is the limit for someone aged 20 in good physical condition, and uses this as a base. To find your own limit, before beginning an exercise programme to get fit, add 40 to your age then subtract this from 200; this is your safe pulse rate and not to be exceeded in the first few weeks. As you become fitter you can slowly take the 40 figure down. Thus, the highest pulse rate a person aged 40 should aim for, when super fit, is 160.

You will find your pulse by placing the fingers of your left hand on the inside of your right wrist, near the base of the thumb, and it is easier to time it if your watch has a second hand.

Three stages of a group race – to the net and back a set number of times. (Spot the understandable cheat!) ▶

▼ Sit-ups: lie flat, touch the court behind you, then sit up and with one hand touch the opposite foot. Repeat with the other hand. Keep your knees slightly bent

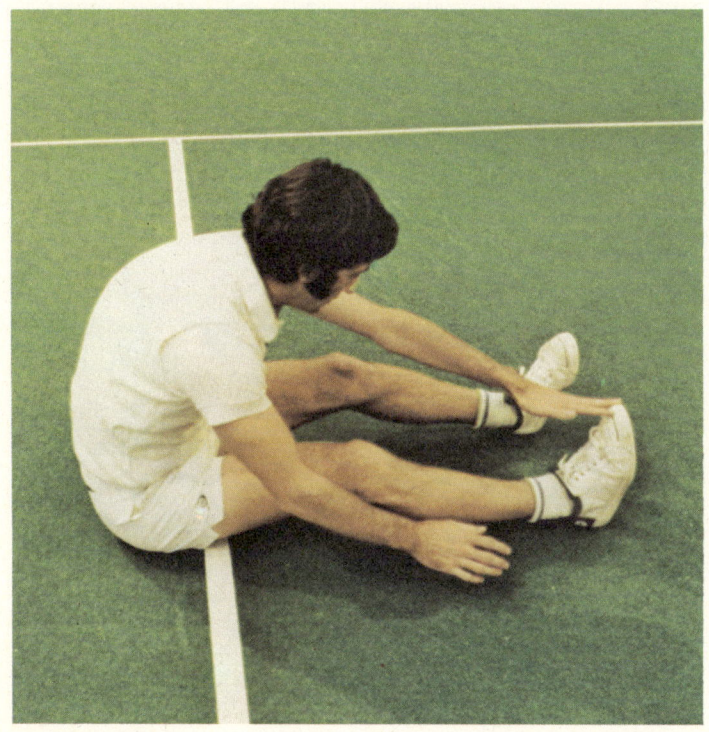

▲ Pull each knee in turn up to your chest; this loosens the muscles in your groin

▼ To loosen your shoulder muscles, rotate an arm forwards for a number of times, then backwards. Then repeat the exercise with the other arm

Tennis requires strength in wrists, arms, shoulders and legs, plus flexibility of the upper part of the body. You can improve your grip, as did Rod Laver, by squeezing an old tennis ball for 10 seconds at a time. Arm and elbow strength can be improved with press-ups (supporting yourself, face down, on hands and feet, hands by shoulders, lifting and lowering your trunk by bending and straightening your elbows). Runs can improve your endurance, but put in 11-16m (10-15yd) sprints every 218m (200yd); do quite a lot of sprinting, for if you are fit but not quite fast enough to reach the ball you will not win at tennis. On these pages (100-103) are illustrated other useful exercises.

A great deal of training can be achieved by three people on court doing pressure training tennis (see page 40): two at the back against one at the net; two at the net playing one at the base line. Finish off with a run before the luxury of a shower.

Before playing tennis endeavour to warm up with exercises; this reduces the possibility of muscle or heart injury and probably leads to a better performance.

Remember, if you wish to stay match fit and, on any day, cannot get on court, do some exercises and go for a run.

▲ Salmon snaps: lie flat, lift your head and legs (legs straight as possible) then lie flat again

Right: More sit-ups as page 101 but touching both feet. ▶
Below: With head and feet up, alternately 'run' and stretch your legs straight and wide

▼ For the upper part of the body: with bent arms, pull back your elbows, then swing back straight arms

Equipment

The three most important pieces of equipment are racket, shoes and balls.

Rackets can have frames of steel, wood or very expensive carbon fibre. A wooden racket is slightly slower through the air than steel but is generally accepted to give more control to ground strokes. Carbon fibre in theory gives both control and speed. For most of us, wood is ideal, as can be seen from the number of top players who win tournaments with wood rackets.

A racket can have either gut or synthetic strings. Gut is a natural fibre and once you are hitting the 'sweet spot' – the area which gives most response – you will gain more 'feel' from gut. Gut is expensive and wears out more quickly, particularly if used in damp conditions. If you have a gut-strung racket, you should have a spare synthetic-strung one (preferably on the same model) for when you play on a damp court with damp balls. Until you become very proficient you should not have a too-tightly strung racket.

In weight, generally speaking, a woman will need a light or light medium, and a man a medium or top weight, racket. The right grip size for your hand is important: too small a grip can cause tennis elbow, too large a one can make your grip insecure. If you are in doubt, your local tennis professional or a reputable sports shop will be able to advise you on grip size, balance and weight. You will need a good press in which to store a wood frame to prevent warping. Take great care of your racket; don't scrape its tip picking up balls from the court nor prop it head down on the grass. If a string goes, get it repaired as soon as possible.

Choose shoes with care; they should be comfortable, fasten securely on your feet, be sturdy and have ribbed soles for a good grip. Flimsy shoes can cause blisters.

The tennis balls you play with should be in good condition. They are made of a rubber core covered with a fluffy wool and nylon skin. Do not expect to get very much control or spin on a ball whose nap has worn smooth. Old balls also lose pressure and become soft. If you are only an occasional player it might be better to buy pressureless balls, which, although not so responsive, will take a long time to go soft.

Always wear smart clothes to go on court. Many clubs and tournaments still stipulate that garments must be predominantly white,

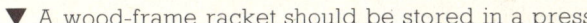

◄ Some of the various sizes and types of racket obtainable, suitable for players from age four upwards. Weight, balance and grip size are all factors to consider

▲ The top players take a good supply of rackets on court

▼ A wood-frame racket should be stored in a press

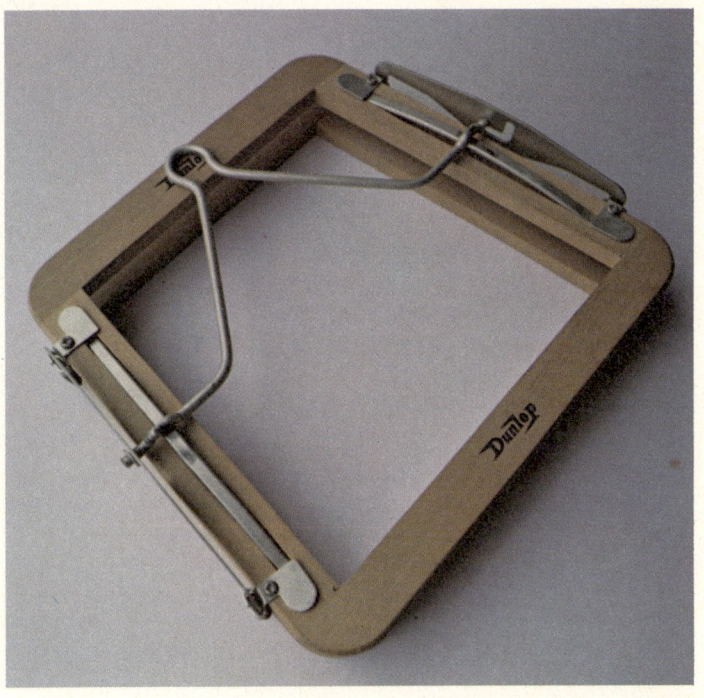

although a number allow players to wear the latest range of pastels. Should you be playing several matches in a day, take a spare set of clothing with you.

There are many possible extras – track suits to keep you warm during the preliminary knock-up, sweat bands, head bands, towelling and gauze grips if your hand slips on the normal leather handle, protective covers for your rackets.

You will notice that world-class players also take on court drinks, sawdust for wiping their grips, spare shoelaces, adhesive plasters for blisters, handkerchiefs and towels – all necessities for today's top players.

You will still lose occasionally to a player with a ten-year-old racket, shoes which should have been thrown away two seasons ago, long shirt sleeves and shorts down over his knees . . . Perhaps equipment does not make a player; but it helps!

▼ Next to his racket, the most important part of a player's equipment is a pair of clean, comfortable, well-fitting shoes, with good gripping soles, which should be reasonably substantial to prevent tired feet and blisters. Remember, your shoes will get pretty tough treatment

▲ Above, left above and right: Standard gear – sweaters, shirts, shorts or skirt (or a dress) and socks plus track suit for a cold day. Although your clothes should allow you freedom of movement, they should not billow and get in your way on a windy day

▲ Stan Smith, serving with one of the latest carbon fibre rackets with a distinctively-shaped head

◀ A headband controls the hair, and keeps any perspiration from trickling down into the eyes

◀ A sweatband on your wrist can keep your hand from getting unduly sweaty, or be used to mop your forehead

How to win (or lose) a match

When the press quotes some of the enormous prizes a tournament player can win, remember that to reach this standard takes many years and a good deal of self-discipline.

The amusing diagrams on these two pages show some of the things you should *not* do if you want to win matches. There are many other things to help or hinder.

The first essential is to enjoy your tennis. If you let it become a chore, some of the zest will disappear from your game.

It is important to play a variety of players; those you can beat, those of the same ability as yourself, and those you can beat easily. Don't evade the latter – all of us were learners once; besides, it will give you the opportunity to play strokes you would not try against a better player.

You can learn a lot, too, from playing those better than yourself, but be prepared to run, chase and try for everything, or your opponent will think it a waste of his time.

You must be fit to play your best. Don't look on tennis as a way to keep fit, but keep fit for tennis. Turn to page 100 for suggestions on how to do it.

Improve your technique and tactics by regular coaching from a qualified professional. When you practise, always hit the ball correctly to 'groove' a stroke, as the professionals say; this will enable you to produce the stroke well, automatically, when you are under pressure. Concentrate on your weak strokes so that you become more confident in using them in match play. You will become a better all-round player and be able to vary your game to your liking and to the conditions and your opponent on the day. Improve your concentration, until you are able to think only of the game in which you are playing and be oblivious to all else.

Think positively. Go on court planning how to win and noting the position of the sun and the strength and direction of the wind.

◀ Do not turn down the opportunity to play in a match. It gives the best practice of all and will enable you to play a mixture of talents, and people with whose game you are unfamiliar

◀ If you are to play really well it is no use to rely on tennis to keep you fit. For instance, the better player on court will run round less. You need a keep-fit programme of running and specific exercises

◀ You will not improve your game sitting in front of the television every evening. Get outside and hit some tennis balls or, if this is not possible, go for a good run

◀ If you arrive late on court for a match you will be hot, bothered and harrassed and liable to be a set down before you pull yourself together

Endeavour to play within your capabilities. If your opponent is a serve-and-volley man, don't try to play the same game if your service is weak or you cannot volley well. Likewise, if your opponent enjoys hitting the cover off the ball and is better at that type of game than you, there can be no point in trading blows with him; you must be the more consistent, and have patience, to beat this type of player. Accept that he will hit winners, but he will also make a lot of mistakes.

Put into every match the utmost effort of which you are capable. If you have tried your best to win every point and still lost, you will have got an enormous amount of enjoyment out of it and will have lost to the better player on the day, never a cause for regret.

Finally, don't give yourself an unrealistic aim or schedule. You may not be able to devote to tennis the time needed to win championships, but you may still do well at club or county level.

▼ Ilie Nastase, one of the most talented players ever, who may well be better remembered for incidents on court

If you celebrate your success at the club bar and stay late while basking in congratulations, make the most of it – because probably you will lose tomorrow! ▶

Before a match, check that your racket strings are in good shape and not frayed and fragile. If you can, take a spare racket with you in case a string breaks during the match, or some other disaster strikes ▶

A loose shoe, a broken lace, a sole coming away from the upper – all can trip you. A shoe sole worn smooth can make you lose your footing. Shoes are your second most important item of equipment. Discard them when they show signs of wear ▶

Be meticulous in packing the equipment for your match. Borrowed gear (if you can get it to fit) takes some getting used to, and habitual borrowers become a bore as well as probable match-losers ▶

Be conversant with all the rules of the game so that no embarrassing – and off-putting – arguments can arise during a match. Know what the score is always ▶

Lose your temper and you will probably lose the game. Remain cool and calm throughout the match, whatever the situation ▶

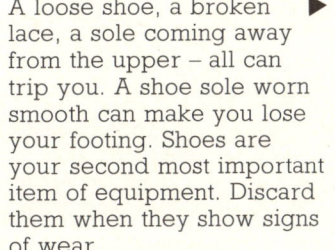

Wimbledon – the dream

Wimbledon is the pinnacle of a player's achievement. That is the verdict of one of the greatest champions, Fred Perry. From far-off Victorian times, when it was the only championship, for more than 100 years, it has been 'The' championship. Even today, when world tennis glitters with glamorous dates, the accolade the superstars strive for is simply 'Wimbledon winner'

Wimbledon was first in the field in 1877 when the All-England Club modestly announced its proposal to hold a lawn tennis meeting open to all amateurs. More than 100 years later, Wimbledon is still first and foremost.

Tennis is one of the greatest spectator sports in the world. Its stars are in the glamorous jet-set, the sport spills dollars by the million and is headline news all the year round. Amid all the ballyhoo stands Wimbledon, retaining its dignity and authority, pre-eminent, the premier tennis championship in the world.

Wimbledon is the one they all want to win. Every year more than 500 men apply to enter. Only 112 are accepted. Others may be invited to play in a qualifying competition from which the last 16 will go into the draw. Only eight of the women invited to qualify for the women's singles

SOUTH WEST HALL

# of every tennis player

will find places in the final 96 in the draw.

Such is the magic of Wimbledon that an unknown rank outsider may have a brief – very brief! – moment of glory opening on the world-famed Centre Court, if the ill-luck of the draw matches him against the previous year's champion. Tradition demands that champions open on the scene of their triumph. That can be a nerve-tingling experience, for fickle Wimbledon has a way of casting aside its champions – as the very first one found out!

Wimbledon actually began in 1868 as the All-England Croquet Club with grounds in Worple Road, Wimbledon, handily near the new railway. One member, Henry Jones, persuaded the committee to set aside a plot for a couple of tennis courts. He was given £25 for equipment,

continued on page 112

Behind the ivy-clad wall on the left lies the Centre Court, used only for the Championship fortnight, then re-sown, nurtured and mollycoddled until next year's Championship. From the balcony is a panoramic view of some of the outside courts where All-England Club members play and where the spectators who cannot squeeze into the Centre Court and No 1 can see all the action and even some of the top stars in close-up

Below, what it's all for: the massive plate presented to the women's singles winner; and, at the foot of the page, the most coveted prize in world tennis: the men's singles Challenge Cup

Wimbledon – the dream of every tennis player

continued from page 111

drew up the rules – which have since hardly changed – refereed the first tournament and even provided the bathroom accommodation at his own expense.

In July, 1877, a crowd of 200 saw Old Harrovian Spencer Gore become the first Wimbledon Men's Singles Champion. The following year a slightly larger crowd saw Gore toppled; and lurking in the shadows was the first of Wimbledon's great champions: Willie Renshaw. For close on a decade Willie and his twin brother Ernest dominated the tournament, crowds flocked to see them and the reputation of Wimbledon grew. After the Renshaws came the Baddeley twins, then the Docherty brothers, but British domination of the native competition ended in 1909 when another Gore – Arthur Wentworth – won his third title at the age of 41. He is still the oldest winner.

It was 25 years before another British player won again: Fred Perry, champion in 1934, 1935 and 1936, the first to win three titles in a row since the abolition of the Challenge Round (when the previous year's champion had to play only the finalist) in 1922, a record that stood until Bjorn Borg's third triumph in 1978.

In 1884, Wimbledon staged its first women's singles. The champion of the first two years was

The march of progress . . . from the intimate, almost garden-party atmosphere of Worple Road (above) in the early days of Wimbledon, to the action-packed tension of the Centre Court today (right), where Virginia Wade serves to Judy Dalton of Australia ▶

▲ A royal occasion for the doubles team of Bob Hewitt and Frew McMillan who hold aloft the championship trophy. The royal family have long been patrons of Wimbledon. The Duke of Kent succeeded his mother, Princess Marina, as president of the All-England Club in 1968

Maud Watson, whose genteel underarm game paved the way for the incomparable Suzanne Lenglen, the redoubtable Helen Wills Moody, Dorothy Round, Louise Brough and perhaps the greatest of all women's champions, Maureen Connolly, winner in 1952, 1953 and 1954, before her career was cut short by a riding accident. 'Little Mo' never lost a singles at Wimbledon. In three magic years she became one of its legends.

In 1922 the All-England Club had moved from overcrowded Worple Road to its present site in Church Road, Wimbledon. Between the wars, the prestige and importance of the tournament grew in the days of 'Big Bill' Tilden, the French musketeers, Borotra, Cochet and Lacoste, and the British triumphs of Perry and Dorothy Round. After the war, Wimbledon led the advocates of 'open' tennis (that is, open to amateurs and professionals alike), which eventually came in 1968 with the return of the big names – to the advantage of the game.

Of course, all has not been smooth: 'shocking' displays of bare legs in the 30s, of frilly panties in the 50s; the professionals quitting in 1972 and 1973, but coming back in 1974; demands by women for prize-money parity, politely turned down – and they played on; threatened political walk-outs averted.

For Wimbledon Championships are bigger than the personalities they create. To play is an honour. To win is the supreme achievement.

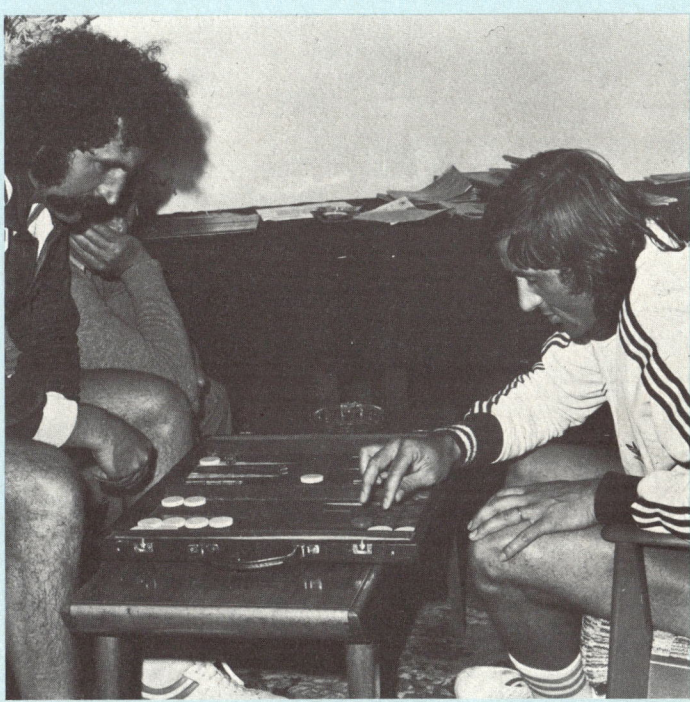

▲ Tensions build up for the top stars like temperamental Ilie Nastase, who relaxes with his fellow-Romanian Ion Tiriac over a game of backgammon. Nastase has been US, French and British Hard Courts champion, but the big one at Wimbledon has always eluded him

Court surfaces

The ones you are most likely to meet:

Grass is the original outdoor surface. If well-maintained, it is still the ideal fine-weather court. It gives a low bounce and a fast game.

Loose shale needs a lot of maintenance, and frost can put it out of action. Bounce is higher than on grass; because of its loose surface, you can slide into a shot.

Tarmacadam-type is usually preferred for public courts as it needs little maintenance. It is very hard, making a slow game, and the balls bounce too high for an enthusiast.

Porous court, recently developed, can be used even in rain. It is costly to lay, has a fairly high bounce, and no 'give', but it is often used indoors as it gives such a reliable bounce.

Wood is the original indoor surface. The ball comes off it very fast, with a low bounce.

Carpet is used indoors. It gives a low bounce, but speed varies with the make, the thickness, the amount of glue used, and the type of surface on which it is laid.

Research continues for a non-maintenance, porous, outdoor court which will play similarly to grass, with a soft surface and low bounce.

Five court surfaces. Below, loose shale – properly rolled and maintained, probably the best hard court. Right, a portable rolled-down carpet court laid at Wembley (Rod Laver, the player). Top, left to right: Wimbledon's peerless grass, a smooth all-weather surface with a different colour surround; a tarmacadam-type public court

Benefits from coaching

There are various ways in which you can improve your tennis. You can watch major tennis events on television, or visit a tournament to savour the atmosphere and pick up ideas at first hand. You can play matches, practise individual shots and gain help from books on tennis.

However, correct techniques and tactics are difficult to acquire on your own, and coaching at the right stage can work wonders.

Ideally, you should start playing tennis as young as possible (America has a national Under Seven championship!) and to swing a racket at the age of four is not unusual these days. To begin with, it is enough to let the little ones accompany Mum and Dad to the club or park and hit balls around with one of the tiny rackets obtainable. The parents can feed balls as shown in the sequence on page 18, but should only do so if the children really want it.

As a child gets older, he can join in some group coaching at the club with a qualified coach. This allows him to play with children of the same age and to have his basic technique sorted out, to be given different practices to try, and generally have a lot of fun.

As an adult beginner, you should start straight

▼ A group coaching session, during which the coach moves round spending a few minutes with each learner

▼ A ball machine projects balls at varying heights, speeds and directions

away with group coaching to get your technique on the right path, and enable you to meet other players with whom to arrange games.

When you (or your child) become a real enthusiast, this is the time to have individual coaching. The coach can concentrate on particular shots which need improving, he will discover which practices will benefit you most, suggest tactics for the type of game you play, and encourage you to play in suitable tournaments.

Neither parents nor coach should pressure a child to play for improvement rather than pleasure. Parents should, of course, take an interest and give their child every opportunity to improve, but they should leave the commitment to him. If they try to produce a champion, they may well produce the type of player who, in his teens, will rebel against playing seven days a week under his parents' watchful gaze, and give it up.

Whatever standard you have reached in the game, a qualified coach can improve it. If you are not sure where to find one, write to the Professional Tennis Coaches' Association, whose address is given on page 125.

▼ The author checks the grip of a left-handed learner. Correct technique learned early on is there for life

▼ The author helps a learner through the motions of a net volley – push, with firm wrist and racket head up

Court manners and customs

Sometimes one sees the unedifying spectacle on court of a player swearing, throwing rackets, banging balls around or arguing with the umpire or linesmen. Don't ever let this be you – or your kids. Control of temperament gives better results and more enjoyment.

There are certain courtesies to observe. If a club rule says that clothing should be predominantly white, wearing your rugby kit is not quite what is meant! Arrive on time for matches, and if it is a home match, be there to greet the visitors and don't rush off immediately after the match.

When serving, start with two balls (even if one is in your pocket), so that you don't have to rout around for another between services. Don't hit an incorrect service back into play, but either let it go or hit it into the bottom of the net. If your partner's first service goes into the net, pick up the ball or push it close to the net, out of the way.

If you hit a lucky winner – a ball that grazes the net and just drops over, or that comes off the frame of your racket, or has a bad bounce – apologize. If you don't agree with a call, play a let; if it was your call and you were late making it, concede the point.

If you lose, don't make excuses. If you win, be pleasant to the loser and take him to the bar for the customary refreshing drink.

The end of a match – Ashe, Tanner, Hewitt and McMillan ▶
shake hands all round, then they will thank the umpire

▼ In mixed doubles, the ladies cross over sides first

▲ A ball has been left on court and could interfere with the rally – especially if you tread on it!

▲ If the first ball served doesn't go over the net, it is the server's partner's job to pick it up

▲ To keep the game running smoothly, the server's partner should help provide her with balls

The rules

The complete Rules of Tennis as approved and published by the International Tennis Federation are obtainable from the various tennis associations (addresses page 125). Here are some of the main ones you will need when you start playing tennis. Those omitted mainly concern the construction and fittings of a court, regulations on the constitution of balls and of rackets, what should be done when rules are infringed, and rules applying to tournaments on such things as allowable rest periods and ball changes.

5 The players shall stand on opposite sides of the net; the player who first delivers the ball shall be called the Server, and the other the Receiver.

6 The choice of ends and the right to be Server or Receiver in the first game shall be decided by toss. The player winning the toss may choose or require his opponent to choose:—
   (a) The right to be Server or Receiver, in which case the other player shall choose the end; or
   (b) The end, in which case the other player shall choose the right to be Server or Receiver.

7 The service shall be delivered in the following manner. Immediately before commencing to serve, the Server shall stand with both feet at rest behind (i.e. further from the net than) the base line, and within the imaginary continuations of the centre mark and side line. The Server

shall then project the ball by hand into the air in any direction and before it hits the ground strike it with his racket, and the delivery shall be deemed to have been complete at the moment of the impact of the racket and the ball. A player with the use of only one arm may utilize the racket for the projection.

8 The Server shall throughout the delivery of the service:—
   (a) Not change his position by walking or running.
   (b) Not touch, with either foot, any area other than that behind the base line within the imaginary extension of the centre mark and side line.

NOTE: The following interpretation of Rule 8 was approved by the International Federation on 9th July, 1958:—

8 (a) The Server shall not, by slight movement of the feet which do not materially affect the location originally taken up by him, be deemed 'to change his position by walking or running'.

   (b) The word 'foot' means the extremity of the leg below the ankle.

9 (a) In delivering the service, the Server shall stand alternately behind the right and left Courts beginning from the right in every game. If service from a wrong half of the Court occurs and is undetected, all play resulting from such wrong service or services shall stand, but the inaccuracy of station shall be corrected immediately it is discovered.

   (b) The ball served shall pass over the net and hit the ground within the Service Court which is diagonally opposite, or upon any line bounding such Court, before the Receiver returns it.

10 The Service is a fault:
   (a) If the Server commit any breach of Rules 7, 8 or 9;
   (b) If he miss the ball in attempting to strike it;
   (c) If the ball served touch a permanent fixture (other than the net, strap or band) before it hits the ground.

11 After a fault (if it be the first fault) the Server shall serve again from behind the same half of the Court from which he served that fault, unless the service was from the wrong half, when, in accordance with Rule 9, the Server shall be entitled to one service only from behind the other half. A fault may not be claimed after the next service has been delivered.

12 The Server shall not serve until the Receiver is ready. If the latter attempt to return the service, he shall be deemed ready. If, however, the Receiver signify that he is not ready, he may not claim a fault because the ball does not hit the ground within the limits fixed for the service.

13 In all cases where a let has to be called under the rules, or to provide for an interruption to play, it shall have the following interpretations:—
   (a) When called solely in respect of a service that one service only shall be replayed.
   (b) When called under any other circumstances, the point shall be replayed.

The rules

14 The service is a let:—
 (a) If the ball served touch the net, strap or band, and is otherwise good, or, after touching the net, strap or band, touch the Receiver or anything which he wears or carries before hitting the ground.
 (b) If a service or a fault be delivered when the Receiver is not ready (see Rule 12).

In case of a let, that particular service shall not count, and the Server shall serve again, but a service let does not annul a previous fault.

15 At the end of the first game the Receiver shall become Server, and the Server Receiver; and so on alternately in all the subsequent games of a match. If a player serve out of turn, the player who ought to have served shall serve as soon as the mistake is discovered, but all points scored before such discovery shall be reckoned. If a game shall have been completed before such discovery, the order of service remains as altered. A fault served before such discovery shall not be reckoned.

16 The players shall change ends at the end of the first, third and every subsequent alternate game of each set, and at the end of each set unless the total number of games in such set be even, in which case the change is not made until the end of the first game of the next set.

17 A ball is in play from the moment at which it is delivered in service. Unless a fault or let be called it remains in play until the point is decided.

18 The Server wins the point:
 (a) If the ball served, not being a let under Rule 14, touch the Receiver or anything which he wears or carries, before it hits the ground.
 (b) If the Receiver otherwise loses the point as provided by Rule 20.

20 A player loses the point if:
 (a) He fail, before the ball in play has hit the ground twice consecutively, to return it directly over the net (except as provided in Rule 24 (a) or (c)); or
 (b) He return the ball in play so that it hits the ground, a permanent fixture, or other object, outside any of the lines which bound his opponent's Court (except as provided in Rule 24 (a) and (c)); or
 (c) He volley the ball and fail to make a good return even when standing outside the Court; or
 (d) He touch or strike the ball in play with his racket more than once in making a stroke; or
 (e) He or his racket (in his hand or otherwise) or anything which he wears or carries touch the net, posts, singles sticks, cord or metal cable, strap or band, or the ground within his opponent's Court at any time while the ball is in play; or
 (f) He volley the ball before it has passed the net; or
 (g) The ball in play touch him or anything that he wears or carries, except his racket in his hand or hands; or
 (h) He throws his racket at and hits the ball.

22 A ball falling on a line is regarded as falling in the Court bounded by that line.

23 If the ball in play touch a permanent fixture (other than the net, posts, singles sticks, cord or metal cable strap or band) after it has hit the ground, the player who struck it wins the point; if before it hits the ground, his opponent wins the point.

24 It is a good return:
 (a) If the ball touch the net, posts, singles sticks, cord or metal cable, strap or band, provided that it passes over any of them and hits the ground within the Court; or
 (b) If the ball, served or returned, hit the ground within the proper Court and rebound or be blown back over the net, and the player whose turn it is to strike reach over the net and play the ball, provided that neither he nor any part of his clothes or racket touch the net, posts, singles sticks, cord or metal cable, strap or band or the ground within his opponent's Court, and that the stroke be otherwise good; or
 (c) If the ball be returned outside the post, or singles stick, either above or below the level of the top of the net, even though it touch the post or singles stick, provided that it hits the ground within the proper Court; or
 (d) If a player's racket pass over the net after he has returned the ball, provided the ball pass the net before being played and be properly returned; or
 (e) If a player succeeds in returning the ball, served or in play, which strikes a ball lying in the Court.

26 If a player wins his first point, the score is called 15 for that player; on winning his second point, the score is called 30 for that player; on winning his third point, the score is called 40 for that player, and the fourth point won by a player is scored game for that player except as below:—

If both players have won three points, the score is called deuce; and the next point won by a player is scored advantage for that player. If the same player win the next point, he wins the game; if the other player wins the next point the score is again called deuce; and so on, until a player wins the two points immediately following the score at deuce, when the game is scored for that player.

27 A player (or players) who first wins six games wins a set; except that he must win by a margin of two games over his opponent and where necessary a set shall be extended until this margin be achieved.

28 The maximum number of sets in a match shall be 5, or, where women take part, 3.

29 Except where otherwise stated, every reference in these Rules to the masculine includes the feminine gender.

30 In matches where an Umpire is appointed, his decision shall be final; but where a Referee is appointed, an appeal shall lie to him from the decision of an Umpire on a question of law, and in all such cases the decision of the Referee shall be final.

In matches where assistants to the Umpire are appointed (Linesmen, Net-cord Judges, Foot-fault Judges) their decisions shall be final on questions of fact except that if in the opinion of an Umpire a clear mistake has been made he shall have the right to change the decision of an assistant or order a let to be played. When such an assistant is unable to give a decision he shall indicate this immediately to the Umpire, who shall give a decision. When an Umpire is unable to give a decision on a question of fact he shall order a let to be played.

In Davis Cup matches or other team competitions where a Referee is on Court, any decision can be changed by the Referee, who may also authorize an Umpire to order a let to be played.

The Referee, in his discretion, may at any time postpone a match on account of darkness or the condition of the ground or the weather. In any case of postponement the previous score and previous occupancy of Courts shall hold good, unless the Referee and the players unanimously agree otherwise.

32 During a match a player may not receive any coaching or advice except that when a player changes ends he may receive instruction from a Captain who is sitting on the Court in a team competition.

The Doubles Game
34 The above Rules shall apply to the Doubles Game except as below.

36 The order of serving shall be decided at the beginning of each set as follows:—

The pair who have to serve in the first game of each set shall decide which partner shall do so and the opposing pair shall decide similarly for the second game. The partner of the player who served in the first game shall serve in the third; the partner of the player who served in the second game shall serve in the fourth, and so on in the same order in all the subsequent games of a set.

37 The order of receiving the service shall be decided at the beginning of each set as follows:—

The pair who have to receive the service in the first game shall decide which partner shall receive the first service, and that partner shall continue to receive the first service in every odd game throughout that set. The opposing pair shall likewise decide which partner shall receive the first service in the second game and that partner shall continue to receive the first service in every game throughout that set. Partners shall receive the service alternately throughout each game.

40 The service is a fault as provided for by Rule 10, or if the ball touch the Server's partner or anything which he wears or carries; but if the ball served touch the partner of the Receiver, or anything which he wears or carries, not being a let under Rule 14 (a) before it hits the ground, the Server wins the point.

41 The ball shall be struck alternately by one or other player of the opposing pairs, and if a player touches the ball in play with his racket in contravention of this rule, his opponents win the point.

Glossary of terms

Advantage: The score call after deuce – advantage server or advantage receiver (see Rule 26, page 123). In friendly games, sometimes called advantage in or advantage out.

Approach shot: Stroke the player makes to prepare for his advance to the net.

Backhand court: Facing the net, the left hand quarter of the court.

Break point: Normally a player wins his service game. If he comes within a point of losing it, that is break point. Hence service break – the receiver winning the game; and break back, the receiver, having just lost his service, wins his opponent's service game.

Closed racket face: The racket face tilted down from the horizontal.

Deuce: The score call if 40-all is reached.

Double fault: Two consecutive service faults from the same position.

Drop shot: Hit with acute underspin for the ball to go just over the net and die (see page 74).

Fault: An incorrect service.

Foot fault: Where the server's foot or feet transgress the rules (Rules 7 or 8, page 120).

Forehand court: Facing the net, the right hand quarter of the court.

Ground stroke: A shot hit from and to the back of the court after the ball has bounced.

Half-volley: A ball hit before it has time to rise more than about 15cm (6in) from its bounce (see page 68).

Let: A call indicating that the service or the point is to be replayed (see Rule 13, page 121).

Line ball: A ball that falls on the relevant line so is still in play.

Lob: A skied ball (see page 70).

Love: A nil score.

Match: The best of three sets or, sometimes in a men's match, of five.

Net-cord: When a ball hits the top of the net before going over it.

Open racket face: The racket face tilted back from the horizontal.

Panel coach: A coach appointed by the LTA to take courses teaching players to become coaches.

Rally: Shots played consecutively for one point.

Serve-volley game: The tactics of the player who tries to win all his points off service or volleys from the net.

Set: When one side has won six games, or if five-all is reached, a margin of two games except when a tie-break is in operation.

Singles sticks: Used to prop the net between the tramlines to bring it to the right height at this point for a singles match.

Tie-break: Instituted sometimes to curtail sets. More than one version. At Wimbledon it operates at eight-games-all (except in a final set). The player who first wins seven points wins the set providing he leads by a margin of two points. At six-points-all the game is extended until this margin is reached. The score is called in ordinary numerals. Except for the first service, each player in turn serves for two points. Ends are changed after every six points.

Tramlines: The pair of side lines (singles side line and doubles side line).

Volley: The ball hit before it bounces.

Useful addresses

GREAT BRITAIN
The Lawn Tennis Association, Barons Court, West Kensington, London W14 9EG.
The Scottish LTA, 7 Albany, Edinburgh EH1 3PY.
The Welsh LTA, The National Sports Centre for Wales, Sophia Gardens, Cardiff.
British Women's Tennis Association, Beaconsfield School of Lawn Tennis, The Oval, Beaconsfield, Bucks.
Girls Schools Association, Cobblers, East Shalford Lane, Guildford.
Boys Schools Association, 50 Royal Hospital School, Ipswich, Suffolk.
Professional Tennis Coaches' Association, 21 Glencairn Court, Lansdown Road, Cheltenham, Gloucestershire GL50 2NB.
'Wimbledon': All England Lawn Tennis and Croquet Club, Church Road, Wimbledon, London SW19 5AE.

UNITED STATES
The United States Tennis Association Incorporated, 51 East 42nd Street, New York, NY 10017.

AUSTRALIA
Lawn Tennis Association of Australia, Box 343, South Yarra, Victoria 3141.

Acknowledgments

The publishers would like to thank the individuals and organizations listed below for their kind permission to reproduce the following photographs in this book:

Arthur and Michael Cole of Le-Roye Productions: page 10; page 28; page 29 (bottom centre); page 30; page 31; page 44; page 45; page 58; page 59; page 60; page 61; page 62; page 75; page 77; page 79 (top); page 80; page 81 (main picture, bottom right); page 82 (main picture, top left, top centre); page 83; page 96; page 97; page 98; page 99 (right, bottom left); page 105 (top); page 108; page 110; page 111; page 113; page 118.
Mary Evans Picture Library: page 29 (left, top right).
Ann Jones: page 98 (top left).
Steven Williams: page 29 (bottom right); page 104.

The following special features were contributed by **Jack Hutchieson:**
The changing face of tennis
Portrait of a superstar
The ladies of the court
The men who make the headlines
The elusive Grand Slam
Wimbledon – the dream of every tennis player